A Radical View:
The "Agate" Dispatches of
Whitelaw Reid
1861-1865

A Radical View:
The "Agate" Dispatches of
WHITELAW REID,
1861-1865

VOLUME TWO

Edited with an Introduction
and Notes by

JAMES G. SMART

MEMPHIS STATE UNIVERSITY PRESS
MEMPHIS, TENNESSEE

Library of Congress Cataloging in Publication Data

Reid, Whitelaw, 1837-1912.
  A radical view.

  1. United States—History—Civil War, 1861-1865—
Personal narratives. 2. United States—History—
Civil War, 1861-1865—Sources. 3. Reid, Whitelaw,
1837-1912. I. Title.
E470.R35 1976   973.7'81   75-20227
ISBN 0-87870-030-7

Vol I—0-87870-031-5
Vol II—0-87870-032-3

Contents
Of Volume Two

VI

Gettysburg

By mid-June 1863 it was apparent that a great battle between Lee's army and the Army of the Potomac was at hand. The *Gazette* accordingly directed Reid to cover the battle. Reid's account was as successful as his effort after Shiloh. The three best newspaper accounts of the battle were by the still unidentified "Bonaparte" of the New York *World*, Charles C. Coffin of the Boston *Journal*, and Reid. "In some aspects Reid's was the best of the three. Its broad sweep, its tense dramatic quality, and its graphic portrayal of the long pauses and sudden outbursts of desperate energy which characterized the struggle marked it as a permanent contribution to the literature of the war."*

Assignment

1863, June 18
From Philadelphia

"Pennsylvania invaded!" "Harrisburg expected to fall!" "Lee's whole army moving through Chambersburg in three grand columns of attack!" And so on for quantity.

*Reprinted from *The North Reports The Civil War* by J. Cutler Andrews (Pittsburgh: University of Pittsburgh Press) 1955, p. 434. By permission of the University of Pittsburgh Press.

1

Such were the pleasing assurances that began to burst on us in the West on Tuesday morning. All Pennsylvania seemed to be quivering in spasms over the invasion. Pittsburgh suspended business and went to fortifying; veracious gentlemen along the railroad lines and in little villages of the interior rushed to the telegraph offices and did their duty to their country by giving their fears to the wings of the lightning. . . .

I was quietly settling myself in comfortable quarters at the Neil House to look on at the counterpart of last week's Vallandigham Convention when dispatches reached me, urging an immediate departure for the scene of action. I was well convinced that the whole affair was an immense panic, but the unquestioned movements of Lee and Hooker have certain promise to something; and besides, whether grounded or groundless, the alarm of invasion was a subject that demanded attention. And so, swallowing my disgust at the irregular and unauthorized demonstrations of the rebels, I hastened off.

A hasty trunk packing and a rush to the depot; and while the delegates to the great Union Convention were gathering by thousands and crowding Columbus as Columbus had never of late been crowded before, save when the people rushed spontaneously to arms at the first call for volunteers, the train was off for Pittsburgh and the East.

Rumors

1863, June 24
From Washington

Washington has become the most *blasé* of cities. She has been "in danger" so long that to be out of danger would give her an unnatural, not to say unpleasant shock.

Just now the indications warrant greater apprehension here than at any point throughout the North; rebel papers incautiously admit that Lee has set out for the capture of Washington and the subjugation of Maryland. The disposition of Hooker's forces seems to warrant the inference that he takes the same view of the rebel plans, and at any rate the whole rebel army is but a short distance from us, and adverse fortunes in the daily expected battle might leave us comparatively at their mercy; yet Harrisburg, Pittsburgh, and even Philadelphia, are frantic, if compared with the unruffled serenity of the Capital. Being in danger pays, and besides, it isn't so very unpleasant a sensation, when you get used to it. . . .

The bulk of Lee's army is still believed to be lying on the west side of Blue Ridge, in the vicinity of Snicker's Gap. Either army is protected in front from the other by the mountain, and matters look very much as if they had reached a deadlock. Some unexpected movement may of course precipitate a collision any hour; or Lee may suddenly dash off on some invading movement that will leave Hooker with a long stern chase before him; but on the other hand there is nothing to make it look improbable that we may have comparative inaction for a month.

While we hold Harper's Ferry and one or two other important points in the neighborhood, an invasion of Southern Pennsylvania is difficult, if not impossible. Lee cannot attack Hooker in front, without forcing the Blue Ridge gaps; if he attempts to ascend the valley and come out on Hooker's flank, he exposes himself on a long flank march, and leaves his transportation and supplies in a hazardous position. Altogether, it begins to look very much as if he had been checkmated in his grand movement of invasion. But,—it is never wise to exult too soon.

1863, June 28
From Washington

I have just returned from a flying visit to Frederick, Maryland. . . .

On the streets of the old fashioned Maryland town I met General Seth Williams, broad faced and genial looking as ever, though the stumpy red beard has sadly changed the familiar appearance of the workingman of McClellan's staff in the earlier days of the war. He had just made fifty miles without leaving the saddle!

From two such instances the movement can be inferred. The energy has been amazing, the rapidity of movement unprecedented in the East, and equaled only by such dashing operations in the West as Mitchell's advance into Alabama. . . .

The week, it would seem, must bring a battle; two days may do it. Our fates depend on no *one* battle now; but if a good Providence shall at last turn the scale in our favor, it will be a sorrier day for rebeldom than defeat of theirs on any field has hitherto proved.

The Battles of Gettysburg

1863, June 29

[Our space this morning is largely occupied with the details of the great battles fought Wednesday, Thursday and Friday of last week, near Gettysburg, Pennsylvania. These reports are from the pen of our well known correspondent Agate, who was on the field, and witnessed all that it was possible for one man to see. As a descriptive writer Agate has few equals, and in addition, he has a merited reputation for reliability that adds largely to the value of his correspondence. We have no space this morning for more than this brief reference to the reports which we spread before our readers.—Cincinnati *Gazette,* July 8, 1863]

Washington, June 29, 1863

Getting a Good Ready

"Would like you (if you feel able) to equip yourself with horse and outfit, put substitutes in your place in the office, and join Hooker's army in time for the fighting."

It was a despatch, Sunday evening, from the manager, kindly alluding to a temporary debility that grew out of too much leisure on a recent visit west. Of course, I felt able, or knew, I should by tomorrow. But, alas! it was Hooker's army no longer. Washington was all a-buzz with the removal. A few idol worshippers hissed their exultation at the constructive disgrace; but for the most part, there

was astonishment at the unprecedented act and indignation at the one cause to which all attributed it. Any reader
who chanced to remember a few paragraphs in a recent
number of the *Gazette,* alluding to the real responsibility
for the invasion, must have known at once that the cause
was—Halleck. How the cause worked, how they quarrelled
about holding Harper's Ferry, how Hooker was relieved in
consequence, and how, within an hour afterward, Halleck
stultified himself by telling Hooker's successor to do as he
pleased concerning this very point, all this will be in print
long before this letter can get west.

For once Washington forgot its *blasé* air, and through a
few hours there was a genuine, old-fashioned excitement.
The two or three Congressmen who happened to be in
town were indignant, and scarcely tried to conceal it; the
crowds talked over the strange affair in all its phases; a
thousand false stories were put in circulation, the basest of
which, perhaps, was that Hooker had been relieved for a
fortnight's continuous drunkenness; rumors of other
charges, as usual, came darkening the very air.

Never before in the history of modern warfare had there
been such a case. A General had brought his army by
brilliant forced marches face to face with the enemy. They
were at the very crisis of the campaign; a great battle,
perhaps the battle of the war, was daily if not hourly
impending. No fault of generalship was alleged, but it
happened that a parlor chieftain in his quiet study three
score miles from the hourly-changing field, differed in
judgment on a single point from the General at the head of
the troops. The later carefully examined anew the point in
issue, again satisfied himself, and insisted on his conviction, or on relief from responsibility for a course he felt

assured was utterly wrong. For this he was relieved—and within five hours was vindicated by his successor.*

But a good, perhaps a better general was put in his place—except from the unfortunate timing of the change, we had good reason to hope it would work, at least no harm. There was little regret for Hooker personally; it was only the national sense of fair play that was outraged.

Presently there came new excitement. Stuart had crossed the Potomac, twenty-five miles from Washington, had captured a train within twelve or thirteen miles, had thrown out small parties to within a mile or two of the railroad between Baltimore and Washington. In the night the road would certainly be cut, and for a few hours at any rate the Capital isolated from the country. We had need to make haste, or it might be difficult "to join Hooker's army."

It was not to be a solitary trip. Samuel Wilkeson, the well-known brilliant writer on the New York *Tribune,* lately transferred to the *Times;* and Uriah H. Painter, chief Washington correspondent of the Philadelphia *Inquirer,* a miracle of energy in such a sphere, were to go; and C. C. Coffin of the Boston *Journal,* known through all New England as "Carleton," had telegraphed an appointment to meet me in the army.

Monday morning Washington breathed freer on learning that the Baltimore trains had come through. Stuart had failed, then? But we counted too fast.

---

*Edwin B. Coddington, *The Gettysburg Campaign,* 1968, pp. 635-36n claims that remarks such as these were responsible for the widely held belief that Hooker was doing well as a military commander, which Coddington effectively challenges, when the Lincoln administration inopportunely relieved him.

A few hasty purchases to make up an outfit for campaigning along the border, and at eleven we were off. Unusual vigilance at the little blockhouses and embankments at exposed points along the road; soldiers out in unusual force, and every thing ready for instant attack; much chattering of Stuart and his failure in the train; anxious inquiries by brokers as to whether communication with New York was to be severed; and so we reach Baltimore.

"Am very sorry, gentlemen; would get you out at once if I could; would gladly run up an extra train for you; but—the rebels cut our road last night, this side of Frederick, and we have no idea when we can run again." Thus Mr. Prescott Smith, whom every body knows, that has ever heard of the Baltimore and Ohio Railroad.

And so Stuart had *not* failed—we were just one train too late and were cut off from the army!

There was nothing for it but to wait; and so—ill satisfied with this "Getting a Good Ready"—back to Washington.

Off

Frederick, Md., Tuesday evening, June 30.

Washington was again like a city besieged as after Bull Run. All night long troops were marching; orderlies with clanking sabres clattering along the streets; trains of wagons grinding over the bouldered avenue; commissaries were hurrying up their supplies; the quartermaster's department was like a beehive; every thing was motion and hurry. From the War Department came all manner of exciting statements; men were everywhere asking what the

President thought of the emergency. Trains had again come through regularly from Baltimore, but how long could it continue? Had not Stuart's cavalry been as near as the old Blair place at Silver Springs, and might they not cut the track any moment they chose? Might they not, indeed, asked the startled bankers, might they not indeed charge past the forts on the Maryland side, pay a hurried visit to the President and Cabinet, and replenish their army chests from *our* well-stored vaults?

In the midst of all this there came a blistering sight that should blacken evermore every name concerned. With cries for reinforcements from the weakened front, with calls for volunteers and raw militia to step into the imminent breach and defend the invaded North, with everywhere urgent need for every man who knew how to handle a musket, there came sprucely marching down the avenue, in all their freshness of brilliant uniforms and unstained arms, with faultlessly appareled officers and gorgeous drum major and clanging band and all the pomp and circumstance of glorious war (about the Capital,) with banners waving and bayonets gleaming in the morning sunlight, as with solid tramp that told of months of drill they moved down the street—in such bravery of peaceful soldiering there came a New England nine months' regiment, mustering over nine hundred bayonets, whose term of service that day expired! With Stuart's cavalry swarming about the very gates of the Capital, with the battle that was to decide whether the war should henceforth be fought on Northern or Southern soil hourly impending, these men, in all the blazonry of banners and music and glittering uniforms and polished arms, were marching—home! They had been implored to stay a fortnight, a week—three days even; but with one accord they insisted on starting *home!* Would that Stuart *could* capture a train that bears them!

Another exciting ride over a yet unmolested track, and we are again in Baltimore. Mr. Prescott Smith gave us the cheering assurance that the road was open again to Frederick; that nobody knew where Stuart had gone, but that in any event they would send us out in the afternoon.

For the rest there was news of more dashing movements by our army. The rebels were reported concentrating at York, Pennsylvania. Our army had already left Frederick far in the rear, and spreading out like a fan to make use of every available road, it was sweeping splendidly up to meet them. There was no fear of their not fighting under Meade. He was recognized as a soldier, brave and able, and they would follow him just as readily as Hooker—some of them indeed, far more willingly. But there was sore need for every musket. Lee at least equalled us in numbers, they thought.

Baltimore had been in a panic. Monday evening some rebel cavalry had ventured up to within a few miles of the city, and frightened persons had rushed in with the story that great squadrons of horse were just ready to charge down the streets. Alarm bells rang, the Loyal Leagues rushed to arms, the thoroughfares were thronged with the improvised soldiery, and within an hour thousands of bayonets guarded every approach. It was worthy the new life of Baltimore. Here, thank God, was an eastern city able and ready at all times to defend itself.

Stuart did not come—if he had, he would have been repulsed.

General Erastus B. Tyler (former Colonel of the Seventh Ohio) had been hastily summoned here to assume command of the defences of Baltimore. This display of citizen soldiery was part of the work he had already done.

But those "defences!" "Small boy," exclaimed Wilkeson as we sauntered through the street and passed an urchin picking pebbles out of a tar barrel to fling at a passing pig, "small boy," and he uttered it with impressive dignity, "You must stop that, sir! You are destroying the defences of Baltimore!" And indeed he was. Single rows of tar barrels and sugar hogsheads, half filled with gravel, and placed across the streets with sometimes a rail or two on top, after the fashion of a "stake and rider" fence, constituted the "defences." They were called barricades, I believe, in some official paper on the subject. Outside the city, however, were earthworks, (to which additions had been made in the press of the emergency,) that would have afforded considerable resistance to an attack; and if cavalry had succeeded in getting into the city, the "barricades" might have been of some service in checking their charges.

In the afternoon Stuart's cavalry was heard from, making the best of its way by a circuitous route on the rear and flank of our army, to join Lee in Southern Pennsylvania. Baltimore, then, was safe; and Stuart had made the most ill advised raid of the war. He had worn out his horses by a terrible march on the eve of a desperate battle when, in the event of a retreat, he was especially needed to protect the rear and hold our pursuit in check; and in return he had gained—a few horses, a single army train which he could only destroy, eighteen hours' interruption of communications by rail between the Capital and the army, and night's alarm in Washington and Baltimore.

Our own army was now reported to be concentrating at Westminister, manifestly to march on York. To reach this point, we must take the Western Maryland road, but this had been abandoned in terror by the Company, and the rolling stock was all in Philadelphia. There was nothing for it but to hasten to Frederick, then mount and follow the track of the army.

As our party stepped into the train a despatch brought Hooker's vindication as against Halleck. He had been relieved for insisting on withdrawing the troops from Harper's Ferry and using them in the active operations of the army. Precisely that thing his successor had done! All honor to Meade for the courage that took the responsibility!

It was a curious ride up the road. Eighteen hours ago the rebels had swarmed across it. The public had no knowledge that they were not yet in its immediate vicinity and might not attack the very train now starting; yet here were cars crowded to overflowing with citizens and their wives and daughters willing to take the risks rather than lose a train. Mr. Smith had been good enough to provide a car for our party, but the press was so great we had to throw open the doors to make room for women and children, recklessly ready to brave what they supposed the dangers of the ride.

Frederick is Pandemonium. Somebody has blundered frightfully; the town is full of stragglers, and the liquor-shops are in full blast. Just under my window scores of drunken soldiers are making night hideous; all over the town they are trying to steal horses or sneak into un-watched private residences or are filling the air with the blasphemy of their drunken brawls. The worst elements of a great army are here in their worst condition; its cowards, its thieves, its sneaks, its bullying vagabonds, all inflamed with whiskey, and drunk as well with their freedom from accustomed restraint.

The Rear of a Great Army

Two Taverns P. O., Pa., July 1.

Our little party broke up unceremoniously. Both my companions thought it better to go back to Baltimore and up to Westminister by rail on the expected Government trains; I thought differently and adhered to the original plan of proceeding overland. I have already good reasons to felicitate myself on the lucky decision.

An hour after breakfast sufficed for buying a horse and getting him equipped for the campaign.

Drunken soldiers were still staggering about the streets, looking for a last drink or a horse to steal, before commencing to straggle along the road, when a messenger for one of the New York papers, who had come down with despatches, and myself were off for headquarters. We supposed them to be at Westminister but were not certain.

South Mountain, historic evermore, since a previous rebel invasion faded out thence to Antietam, loomed up on the left amid the morning mists; before us stretched a winding turnpike, upheaved and bent about by a billowy country that in its cultivation and improvements began to give evidence of proximity to Pennsylvania farmers. The army had moved up the valley of the Monocacy through Walkersville, Woodbury, and Middleburg—all pleasant little Maryland villages—where in peaceful times Rip Van Winkle might have slumbered undisturbed. The direction seemed too far north for Westminister, and a courier, coming back with despatches, presently informed us that headquarters were not there but at Taneytown, a point considerably father north and west. Evidently there was a change in our plans. We were not going to York, or headquarters would not be at Taneytown; and it was fair to suppose that our movements to the northwest were based upon news of a similar concentration by the rebels. The probabilities of a speedy battle were thus immensely increased, and we hastened the more rapidly on.

From Frederick out the whole road was lined with stragglers. I have heard General Marsena R. Patrick highly spoken of as an efficient Provost-Marshal General for the Potomac Army; but if he is responsible for permitting such scenes as were witnessed today in the rear, his successor is sadly needed.

Take a worthless vagabond, who has enlisted for thirteen dollars a month instead of patriotism, who falls out of ranks because he is a coward and wants to avoid the battle, or because he is lazy and wants to steal a horse to ride on instead of marching, or because he is rapacious and wants to sneak about farmhouses and frighten or wheedle timid countrywomen into giving him better food and lodging than camp life affords—make this armed coward or sneak or thief drunk on bad whiskey, give him scores and hundreds of armed companions as desperate and drunken as himself—turn loose this motley crew, muskets and revolvers in hand into a rich country with quiet, peaceful inhabitants, all unfamiliar with armies and army ways—let them swagger and bully as cowards and vagabonds always do, steal or openly plunder as such thieves always will-and then, if you can imagine the state of things this would produce, you have the condition of the country in the rear of our own army on our own soil today.

Of course these scoundrels are not types of the army. The good soldiers never straggle—these men are the *debris*, the offscourings from nearly a hundred thousand soldiers.

There is no need for permitting these outrages. An efficient Provost Marshal, such as General Patrick has been called, would have put a provost guard at the rear of every division, if not of every regiment and brigade, and would have swept up every man that dared to sneak out of ranks when his comrades were marching to meet the enemy. The rebels manage these things better. Death on the spot is said to be their punishment for straggling, and in the main it is a just one.

The army itself had done surprisingly little damage to property along their route. Breaking off the limbs of cherry trees to pick the ripe cherries seemed to be about the worst of their trespasses. I have never before seen the country so little injured along the line of march of a great army.

But every farmhouse was now filled with drunken loafers in uniform; they swarmed about the stables, stealing horses at every opportunity and compelling farmers to keep up a constant watch; in the fence corners groups of them lay, too drunk to get on at all.

As we neared the army a new phase of the evil was developed. A few mounted patrols seemed to have been sent out to gather up the stragglers, and some of them had begun their duty by getting drunk, too.

In one fence corner we passed a drunken trio in fierce altercation with a gay-looking, drunken patrol with a rose jauntily worn in his button-hole and a loaded and cocked revolver carelessly playing in his hand. "These fellows are d-dr-drunk," he explained to us, "and ac'ly talk about sh-shootin' me for or'rin 'em to go to camp." One of the stragglers had his musket cocked and handsomely covering the red rose on the patrol's breast.

A few yards further on was another drunken party

under the trees. A patrol, trying to get them started, was just drunk enough to be indiscreetly brave and talkative. "You're cowardly stragglers, every rascal of you," he roared, after a few minutes' unavailing efforts of coaxing. "You're lyin' scoune'rl," was the thick-tongued response; and the last we saw of the party as we galloped on, two of the stragglers were rushing at the patrol, and he was standing at a charge bayonets, ready to receive them. They probably halted before they reached the bayonet point.

As we stopped at a farmhouse by the roadside to feed our horses and get dinner, we passed a party of stragglers in the yeard. After dinner to our amazement we discovered that my luckless "rebel look"* and an indignant reply about straggling to some impertinent question they had asked, had well-nigh got us into trouble. The rascals, drunk enough to half believe what they said, and angry enough at being called stragglers to do us any mischief they were able, had held a court on our cases while we were eating had adjudged us rebel spies and had sentenced us to—have our horses confiscated! Luckily my companion strolled down to the stable after dinner just as the fellows were getting the horses out to make off with them! They announced their conclusion that we were spies, and their sentence, and insisted on the horses, but a judicious display of hearty disposition on his part to knock somebody down induced them to drop the reins and allow him to put the horses back in the stable.

We had small time, as we galloped through, to appreciate the beauties of Taneytown, a pleasant little Maryland hamlet, named in honor of the Chief Justice of the United

* Reid wore his hair long, "Southern style."

States (who has a countryseat in the vicinity,) and like
him now somewhat fallen into the sere and yellow leaf.
Army trains blocked up the streets; a group of quarter-
masters and commissaries were bustling about the principal
corner; across on the hills and along the road to the left,
far as the eye could reach, rose the glitter from the
swaying points of bayonets as with steady tramp the
columns of our Second and Third corps were marching
northward. They were just getting started—it was already
well on in the afternoon. Clearly something was in the
wind.

Half a mile further east, splashed by the hoofs of eager
gallopers, a large, unpretending camp, looking very much
like that of a battalion of cavalry—we turn in without
ceremony and are at the headquarters of the Army of the
Potomac.

At first all seems quiet enough, but a moment's observation shows signs of movement. The slender baggage is all
packed, everybody is ready to take the saddle at a moment's notice. Engineers are busy with their maps; couriers
are coming in with reports; the trustiest counsellors on the
staff are with the General.

In a plain little wall tent, just like the rest, pen in hand,
seated on a camp-stool and bending over a map, is the new
"General Commanding" for the Army of the Potomac.
Tall, slender, not ungainly, but certainly not handsome or
graceful, thin-faced, with grizzled beard and moustache, a
broad and high but retreating forehead, from each corner
of which the slightly-curling hair recedes, as if giving pre-
monition of baldness-apparently between forty-five and
fifty years of age—altogether a man who impresses you
rather as a thoughtful student than a dashing soldier—so
General Meade looks in his tent.

"I tell you, I think a great deal of that fine fellow Meade," I chanced to hear the President say a few days after Chancellorsville. Here was the result of that good opinion. There is every reason to hope that the events of the next few days will justify it.

A horseman gallops up and hastily dismounts. It is a familiar face—Lorenzo L. Crounse, the well-known chief correspondent of the *New York Times* with the Army of the Potomac. As we exchange hurried salutations, he tells us that he has just returned from a little post village in Southern Pennsylvania, ten or fifteen miles away; that a fight, of what magnitude he cannot say, is now going on near Gettysburg between the First corps and some unknown force of the enemy; that Major General John F. Reynolds is already killed, and that there are rumors of more bad news.

Mount and spur for Gettysburg is, of course, the word. Crounse, who is going too, acts as guide. We shall precede headquarters but a little. A few minutes in the Taneytown tavern porch, writing despatches to be forthwith sent back by special messenger to the telegraph office at Frederick; then in among the moving mass of soldiers and down the Gettysburg road at such speed as we may. We have made twenty-seven miles over rough roads already today; as the sun is dipping in the woods of the western hilltops, we have fifteen more ahead of us.

It is hard work, forcing our way amoung the moving masses of infantry, or even through the crowded trains, and we make but slow progress. Presently aids and orderlies begin to come back, with an occasional quartermaster or surgeon or commissary in search of stores. Crounse seems to know every body in the army, and from every

one he demands the news from the front. "Everything
splendid; have driven them five or six miles from Gettysburg." "Badly cut up, sir, and falling back." "Men rushed
in like tigers after Reynold's death, and swept everything
before them." (Rushing in like tigers is a stock performance, and appears much oftener in the newspapers than
on the field.) "Gettysburg burnt down by the rebels."
"Things were all going wild, but Major General Winfield S.
Hancock got up before we were utterly defeated, and I
guess there's some chance now." "D--d Dutchmen of the
Eleventh corps broke and ran like sheep, just as they did at
Chancellorsville, and it's going to be another disaster of
just the same sort." "We still hold Gettysburg, and everything looks favorable." "Major General James S. Wadsworth's division cut to pieces; not a full regiment left out
of the whole of it; and half the officers killed." "We've
been driven pell-mell through Gettysburg, and things look
bad enough, I tell you."

This is the substance of the information we gain by
diligent questioning of scores. It is of such stuff that the
"news direct form the battlefield," made up by itinerant
liars and "reporters" at points twenty or thirty miles
distant, and telegraphed thence throughout the country, is
manufactured. So long as the public, in its hot haste,
insists on devouring the news before it is born, so long
must it expect such confusion and absurdity.

Riding through the columns became more and more
difficult as we advanced; and finally, to avoid it, we turned
off into a by-way on the right. We were fortunately well
supplied with maps, and from these we learned that but a
few miles to the right of the Taneytown road, up which we
had been going, ran the great Baltimore turnpike to Get-

tysburg; and a Dutch farmer told us that our by-path would bring us out, some miles ahead, on this pike. It was certain to be less obstructed, and we pushed on.

Across the hills to the left we could see the white-covered wagons slowly winding in and out through the forests and the masses of blue coats toiling forward. In either direction for miles you could catch occasional glimpses of the same sight through the openings of the foliage. The shades of evening dimmed and magnified the scene till one might have thought the hosts of Xerxes, in all the glory of modern armor, were pressing on Gettysburg. To the front and right lay broad, well-tilled farms, dotted here and there with mammoth, many windowed barns, covered with herds and rustling with the ripening grain.

Selecting a promising looking Dutch house, with a more than usually imposing barn in its rear, we stopped for supper. The good man's "woman" had gone to see the soldiers on the road, but whatever he could get for us "you be very heartily welcome to." Great cherry trees bent before the door under their weight of ripe fruit; the kitchen garden was crowded with vegetables; contented cattle stood about the barn; sleek horses filled the stables; fat geese hissed a doubtful welcome as we came too near them; the very farmyard laughed with plenty.

We put it on the ground of resting our horses and giving them time for their oats; but I fear the snowy bread and well spread table of the hearty farmer had something to do with the hour that we spent.

Then mount and spur again. It was dark in the woods, but our bypath had become a neighborhood wagon road, and the moon presently cast us occasional glances from behind the clouds. The country was profoundly quiet; the Dutch farmers seemed to have all gone to bed at dark, and only their noisy house dogs gave signs of life as we passed. Once or twice we had to rouse a sleeping worthy out of bed for directions about the road. At last campfires gleamed through the woods; presently we caught the hum of soldiers' talk ahead; by the roadside we passed a house where all the lights were out, but the family were huddled on the doorstep, listening to the soldiers. "Yes, the army's right down there. If you want to stay all night, turn up by the school-house. 'Squire Durboraw's a nice man'."

"Right down there" was the post-village of Two Taverns—thronged with soldiers—the women all in the streets, talking and questioning and frightening themselves at a terrible rate. A corps general's headquarters had been there today, but they were now moved up to the front. That didn't look like serious disaster. We were four miles and a quarter or a half from the line of battle. Ewell had come down from York, and we had been fighting him today. A. P. Hill was also up coming by way of Chambersburg or Hagerstown. Longstreet was known to be on the way and would certainly be here tomorrow. The reserves were on their way. In short, Lee's whole army was rapidly concentrating at Gettysburg, and tomorrow, it seemed, must bring the battle that is to decide the invasion. Today it had opened for us—*not* favorably.

"Squire Durboraw *is* a nice man." We roused him out of bed, where he must have been for two or three hours. "Can you take care of us and our horses till morning?" "I will do it with pleasure, gentlemen." And no more words are needed. The horses are housed in one of those great horse palaces these people build for barns; we are comfortably and even luxuriously quartered. If the situation is as we hope, our army must attack by daybreak. At any rate, we are off for the field at four in the morning.

The Repulse on Wednesday, First July

Field of Battle, near Gettysburgh, July 2

To the Front

We were in the saddle this morning a little after daybreak. The army was cut down to fighting weight; it had shaken off all retainers and followers—all but its fighters; and the road was alive with this useless material.

My companion and myself were forcing our way as fast as possible through the motley crowd toward the front, where an occasional shot could already be heard, and where we momentarily expected the crash of battle to open, when I was stopped by some one calling my name from a little frame dwelling, crowded with wounded soldiers. It proved to be Colonel Luther S. Stephenson, the librarian of Congress. He had run away from his duties in the Capital, and all day yesterday, through a fight that we now know to have been one of the hottest in the war, had been serving most gallantly as aid on General Solomon Meredith's staff. Congress should make an example of its runaway official!

The lower story of the house was crowded with wounded from the old "Iron Brigade" of Wadsworth's division; in a little upper room was their General. He had been grazed on the head with a fragment of shell, his horse had

been shot under him and had fallen upon him; he had
been badly bruised externally and worse internally, and
there was little prospect of his being ready for service again
for months. He spoke proudly of the conduct of his men,
almost tearfully of their unprecedented losses.

Half a mile further on, through crowds of slightly
wounded, and past farmhouses converted into hospitals, a
turn to the right through a meadow, up the slope of an
exposed hill, and by the side of a smouldering camp-fire.
Stretched on the ground, and surrounded by his staff, lies
General Wadsworth, (late Republican candidate for Governor of New York,) commander of the advance division in
yesterday's fight. He, too, kindles as he tells the story of
the day, its splendid fighting, and the repulse before overwhelming numbers.

Batteries are all about us; troops are moving into position; new lines seem to be forming, or old ones extending.
Two or three general officers, with a retinue of staff and
orderlies, come galloping by. Foremost is the spare and
somewhat stooped form of the Commanding General. He
is not cheered, indeed is scarcely recognized. He is an
approved corps General, but he has not yet vindicated his
right to command the Army of the Potomac. By his side is
the calm, honest, manly face of General Oliver O. Howard.
An empty coat sleeve is pinned to his shoulder—memento
of a hard fought field before, and reminder of many a
battle scene his splendid Christian courage has illumined.
They are arranging the new line of battle. Howard's dispositions of the preceding night are adopted for the centre;
his suggestions are being taken for the flanks. It is manifest
already that we are no longer on the offensive, that the
enemy had the initiative.

The Position

A little further forward, a turn to the left, we climb the slope of another hill, hitch our horses halfway up under cover of the woods, make our way through frowning batteries and by long rows of tombstones, stop for an instant to look at the monument of a hero from Fair Oaks, and are startled by the buzzing hiss of a well-aimed Minie from the foes that fought us at Fair Oaks, above our heads, move forward to an ambitious little gate-keeper's lodge at the entrance of the cemetery.

In front on a gradual declivity an orchard of gnarled old leafy trees; beyond the valley, a range of hills but little lower than that on which we stand; on this slope, half hidden among the clusters of trees, a large cupola-crowned brick building—a theological seminary; between this and us half a dozen spires, roofs of houses, distinguishable amid the luxuriant foliage, streets marked by the lines of trees— Gettysburg!

No sound comes up from the deserted town, no ringing of bells, no voices of children, no hum of busy trade. Only now and then a blue curl of smoke rises and fades from some high window; a faint report comes up, and perhaps the hiss of a Minie is heard; the houses are not wholly without occupants.

We are standing on Cemetery Hill, the key to the whole position the enemy occupies, the centre of our line and the most exposed point for a concentration of the rebel fire. To our right and a little back, is the hill on which we have just left General Wadsworth; still farther back and sweeping away from the cemetery almost like the side of a horse-shoe from the toe, is a succession of other hills, some covered with timber and undergrowth, others yellow in the morning sunlight, and waving with luxuriant wheat; all crowned with batteries that are soon to reap other than a wheaten harvest. To the left, our positions are not so distinctly visible; though we can make out our line stretching off in another horse-shoe bend, behind a stone fence near the cemetery—unprotected, farther on; affording far fewer advantageous positions for batteries, and manifestly a weaker line on our right. An officer of General Howard's staff pointed out the positions to me, and I could not help hazarding the prediction that there on our left wing would come the rebel attack we were awaiting.

General Howard's headquarters were on this very Cemetery Hill—the most exposed position on the whole field. He had now returned and was good enough during the lull that still lasted, while we awaited the anticipated attack, to explain the action of yesterday as he saw it.

The Battle of Wednesday

I have now conversed with four of the most prominent generals employed in that action and with any numbers of subordinates. I am a poor hand to describe battles I do not see, but in this case I must endeavor to weave their statements into a connected narrative. The ground of the action is still in the enemy's hands, and I have no knowledge of it save from the description of others, and the distant view one gets from Cemetery Hill.

We had been advancing toward York. It was discovered that the rebels were moving for a concentration farther south, and we suddenly changed our own line of march. The First corps, Major General John F. Reynolds, had the

advance; next came the unfortunate Eleventh corps, with a
new record to make that should wipe out Chancellorsville,
and ready to do it.

Saturday they had been at Boonesboro, twelve or fifteen miles to the northwest of Frederick; by Tuesday
night, the First corps lay encamped on Marsh Creek, within easy striking distance of Gettysburg. The Eleventh
corps was ten or twelve miles farther back. Both were
simply moving under general marching orders, and the
enemy was hardly expected yet for a day or two.

At an early hour in the forenoon the First corps was
filing down around Cemetery Hill in solid column, and
entering the streets of Gettysburg. In the town our skirmishers had met pickets or scouts from the enemy and had
driven them pell-mell back. The news fired the column,
and General Reynolds with little or no reconnoissance
marched impetuously forward. Unfortunate haste of a
hero, gone now to the hero's reward!

It was fifteen minutes past ten o'clock. The fire of the
rebel skirmishers rattled along the front, but shaking it off
as they had the dew from their night's bivouac, the men
pushed hotly on.

Meantime General Reynolds, on receiving his first notice
an hour ago from Brigadier General John Buford's cavalry,
that the rebels were in the vicinity of Gettysburg, had
promptly sent word back to General Howard, and asked
him, as a prudential measure, to bring up the Eleventh
corps as rapidly as possible. The Eleventh had been coming
up on the Emmetsburg road. Finding it crowded with the
train of the First, they had started off on a byway, leading
into the Taneytown road, some distance ahead; and were
still on this byway eleven miles from Gettysburg when

Reynold's messenger reached them. The fine fellows, with stinging memories of not wholly merited disgrace at Chancellorsville, started briskly forward, and a little after one their advance brigade was filing through the town to the music of the fire above. General Reynold's corps consists of three divisions—Wadsworth's, Major General Abner Doubleday's, and Brigadier General John C. Robinson's. Wadsworth's (composed of Brigadier General Solomon Meredith's and Major General Lysander Cutler's brigades—both mainly Western troops) had the advance, with Cutler on the right and Meredith on the left. Arriving at the Theological Seminary above the town, the near presence of the enemy became manifest, and they placed a battery in position to feel him out and gradually moved forward.

An engagement of more or less magnitude was evidently imminent. General Reynolds rode forward to select a position for a line of battle. Unfortunate—sadly unfortunate again—alike for him with all a gallant soldier's possibilities ahead of him and for the country, that so sorely needed his well-trained services. He fell almost instantly, pierced by a ball from a sharpshooter's rifle, and was borne, dying or dead, to the rear. General Doubleday was next in command.

The enemy was seen ready. There was no time to wait for orders from the new corps commander; instantly, right and left, Cutler and Meredith wheeled into line of battle on the double quick. Well tried troops, those; no fear of *their* flinching; veterans of a score of battles—in the war some of them from the very start; with the first at Philippi, Laurel Hill, Carrick's Ford, Cheat Mountain and all the Western Virginia campaign, trusted of Shields at Winchester, and of Lander at Romney and Bloomery Gap;

through the campaign of the Shenandoah Valley, and with the Army of the Potomac in every march to the red slaughter sowing that still had brought no harvest of victory. Meredith's old Iron Brigade was the Nineteenth Indiana, Twenty-fourth Michigan, Sixth and Seventh Wisconsin—veterans all, and well mated with the brave New Yorkers whom Wadsworth also led.

Cutler, having the advance, opened the attack; Meredith was at it a few minutes later. Short, sharp fighting, the enemy handsomely repulsed, three hundred rebel prisoners taken, Brigadier General James J. Archer himself reported at their head—such was the auspicious opening. No wonder the First determined to hold its ground.

Yet they were ill prepared for the contest that was coming. Their guns had sounded the tocsin for the Eleventh, but so they had too for—Ewell, already marching down from York to rejoin Lee. They were fighting two divisions of A. P. Hill's now—numerically stronger than their dwindled three. Their batteries were not up in sufficient numbers; on Meredith's left—a point that especially needed protection, there were none at all. A battery with Buford's cavalry stood near. Wadsworth cut red tape and in an instant ordered it up. The Captain, preferring red tape to red fields, refused to obey. Wadsworth ordered him under arrest, could find no officer for the battery, and finally fought it under a sergeant. Sergeant and captain there should henceforth exchange places.

The enemy repulsed, the First advanced their lines and took the position lately held by the rebels. Very heavy skirmishing, almost developing at times into a general musketry engagement, followed. Our men began to discover that they were opposing a larger force. Their own line, long and thin, bent and wavered occasionally, but bore bravely up. To the left, where the fire seemed the hottest, there were no supports at all, and Wadsworth's division, which had been in the longest, was suffering severely.

About one o'clock Major General Howard, riding in advance of his hastening corps, arrived on the field and assumed command. Carl Schurz was thus left in command of the Eleventh while Doubleday remained temporarily Reynold's successor in the First.

The advance of the Eleventh soon came up and was thrown into position to the right of the First. They had little fighting immediately—but their time was coming. Meantime the First, that had already lost its General commanding and had held its ground against superior numbers, without supports, from ten till nearly two, took fresh courage as another corps came up, and all felt certain of winning the day.

But alas! the old, old game was playing. The enemy was concentrating faster than we. Perhaps no one was to blame for it; no one among the living at least, and the thickly clustering honors that fitly crown the hero's grave bar all criticism and pardon all mistakes, if mistakes they were.

About half-past two that afternoon, standing where we now stand, on Cemetery Hill, one might have seen a long, gray line, creeping down the pike and near the railroad on the northeast side of the town. Little pomp in their march, but much haste; few wagons, but the ammunition trains all up; and the battle flags that float over their brigades are not our flags. It is the road from *York*—these are Stonewall Jackson's men—led now by Stonewall Jackson's most trusted and loved Lieutenant [Ewell]. That gray serpent, bending in and out through the distant hills, decides the day.

They are in manifest communication with Hill's corps, now engaged, fully advised of their early losses, and of the exact situation. They bend up from the York road, debouch in the woods near the crest of the hill, and by three o'clock, with the old yell and the old familiar tactics, their battleline comes charging down.

Small resistance is made on our right. The Eleventh does not flee wildly from its old antagonists, as at their last meeting when Stonewall Jackson scattered them as if they had been pigmies, foolishly venturing into the war of the Titans. It even makes stout resistance for a little while; but the advantage of position, as of numbers, is all with the rebels, and the line is forced to retire. It is done deliberately and without confusion, till they reach the town. Here the evil genius of the Eleventh falls upon it again. To save the troops from the terrible enfilading fire through the streets, the officers wheel them by detachments into cross streets, and attempt to march them thus around one square after another, diagonally, through the town. The Germans are confused by the maneuvre; perhaps the old panic at the battle cry of Jackson's flying corps comes over them; at any rate they break in wild confusion, some pouring through the town [in] a rout, and are with difficulty formed again on the heights to the southward. They lose over one thousand two hundred prisoners in twenty minutes. One of their Generals, Alexander Schimmelfennig, an old officer in the Russian service in the Crimean War, is cut off, but he shrewdly takes to cover, conceals himself somewhere in the town, and finally escapes.

But while our right is thus suddenly wiped out, how

fares it with the left—Robinson, and Doubleday, and sturdy Wadsworth, with the Western troops? Sadly enough.

By half-past three, as they counted the time, the whole of A. P. Hill's corps, acting in concert now with Ewell, precipitated itself upon their line. These men are as old and tried soldiers as there are in the war, and they describe the fire that followed as the most terrific they have ever known. In a single brigade, (Cutler's,) in twenty minutes, every staff officer had his horse shot under him, some of them two and three. In thirty minutes not a horse was left to General or staff, save one, and that one—as if the grim mockery of war there sought to outdo itself—had his tail shot off! General Cutler himself had three horses shot under him.

Few troops could stand it. All of the First corps could not. Presently the thin line of fire began to waver and bend and break under those terrible volleys from the dark woods above. The officers, brave almost always to a fault, sought to keep them in. One—his name deserves to be remembered—Captain Hollon Richardson of the Seventh Wisconsin seized the colors of a retreating Pennsylvania regiment and strove to rally the men around their flag. It was in vain; none but troops that have been tried as by fire can be reformed under such a storm of death; but the captain, left alone and almost in the rebels' hands, held on to the flaunting colors of another regiment, that made him so conspicuous a target, and brought them safely off.

The right of the corps gave way. The fierce surge of Ewell's attack had beaten up to their front, and, added to Hill's heavy fire, forced them slowly back.

Wadsworth still holds on—for a few minutes more his

braves protract the carnival of death. Doubleday managed
to get three regiments over to their support; Colonel James
Biddle's Pennsylvania regiment came in and behaved most
gallantly. Colonel Stephenson, who all the day had been
serving in the hottest of the fight as aid to Meredith,
relieved a wounded colonel, and strove to rally his regiment. Meredith himself, with his Antietam wound hardly
yet ceasing to pain him, is struck again, a mere bruise,
however—on the head, with a piece of shell. At the same
instant his large, heavy horse falls, mortally wounded,
bears the General under him to the ground, and beats him
there with his head and shoulders in his death convulsions.

It is idle fighting Fate. Ewell turned the scale with the
old, historic troops; brave men may now well retire
before double their number equally brave. When the Eleventh corps fell back, the flank of the First was exposed;
when the right of the First fell back, Wadsworth's flank
was exposed; already flushed with their victory, rebels
were pouring up against front and both flanks of the
devoted brigades. They had twice cleared their front of
rebel lines; mortal men could now do no more. And so,
"slowly and sullenly firing," the last of them came back.

Meantime, the fate of the army had been settled. It was
one of those great crisis that come rarely more than once
in a lifetime. For Major General Howard, brave, one-
armed, Christian fighting hero, the crisis had come.

His command—two corps of the Grand Army of the
Potomac—were repulsed, and coming back in full retreat, a
few sturdy brigades in order, the most in sad confusion.
One cavalry charge; twenty minutes' well-directed cannonading, might wipe out nearly a third of the army, and
leave Meade powerless for the defence of the North. These
corps must be saved, and saved at once.

"That road defies description. Part of the time it ran through lanes so narrow that a horseman could not pass on either side of the wagon train; then it wound through mountain gullies where the wheels of the wagon would be on the sides of the opposite hills, while beneath rush a stream of water down the gulley . . . , and then again [it] would seem, in the language of one of the Hoosiers, 'to run clean out.'"
—Agate Dispatch, *July 14, 1861*

NEWSPAPER ROW IN 1873

*—U.S. Bureau of Public Roads, Photo No. 30-N-31-629 in
the National Archives*

A photograph taken in the
1880's of RICHARD SMITH,
Editor of the *Gazette*
"... *I have no particular
penchant for [George] Julian,
I like him because he's honest,
& not a coward. As Mr. Rich'd
Smith is, if he talks about
hesitating to publish anything
because it comes from a
'Radical.' I'm disgusted at
such stupidity. I thought better of him, & am trying still to
persuade myself that you must
be mistaken some way about
it.*"

—Reid to William Henry Smith,
May 23, 1863,
Ohio Historical Society,
Columbus, Ohio

ANNA E. DICKINSON, the North's "Joan of Arc."

"Of course she is radical as all women of culture are likely to be. . . ."
—Agate Dispatch, *June 22, 1863*

The Death of General Robert Selden Garnett, C.S.A.

"In an instant Sergeant Burlingame 'drew a bead' on him and fired."
—Agate Dispatch July 14, 1861

THE REBEL FLEA.
You put your Finger on him, and he isn't there.

"... *Whenever you get a report ... giving glowing accounts of our having* surrounded *the enemy anywhere, set it down as a palpable* canard."
—Agate Dispatch, *March 7, 1862*

PITTSBURGH LANDING.

SECRETARY CHASE'S BRIGADE.

Reid's view of Chase was comparable to the one presented in this Harper's Weekly illustration. Over forty years after the war Reid believed that as an anti-slavery leader and as Chief Justice Chase was rivaled by few others and "that as financier there is no man in the history of the US to be ranked above him, unless it be Alexander Hamilton...."

—Reid to Senator John B. Foraker, Sept. 20, 1906, Reid Paper Library of Congress

General Howard met and overmastered the crisis. The Cemetery Hill was instantly selected. The troops were taken to the rear and reformed under cover. Batteries hurried up, and when the rebel pursuit had advanced halfway through the town a thunderbolt leaped out from the whole length of that line of crest and smote them where they stood. The battle was ended, the corps were saved.

The last desperate attack lasted nowhere along the line over forty minutes; with most of it hardly over half so long. One single brigade, that "iron" column that held the left, went in one thousand eight hundred and twenty strong. It came out with seven hundred men. A few were prisoners; a few concealed themselves in houses and escaped—near a thousand of them were killed and wounded. Its fellow brigade went in one thousand five hundred strong; it came out with forty-nine officers and five hundred and forty-nine men killed and wounded, and six officers and five hundred and eighty-four men missing and their fate unknown. Who shall say that they did not go down into the very valley of the Shadow of Death on that terrible afternoon?

Thursday's Doubtful Issue—Friday's Victory

Field of Battle near Gettysburg, Pa., July 4

Two more days of such fighting as no Northern State ever witnessed before, and victory at last! Victory for a fated army, and salvation for the imperilled country!

It were folly for one unaided man, leaving the ground within a few hours after the battle has died fitfully out, to undertake a minute detail of the operations on all parts of the field. I dare only attempt the merest ouline of its leading features—then off for Cincinnati by the speediest routes.

I have been unable even to learn all I sought concerning the part some of our own Ohio regiments bore—of individual brigades and regiments and batteries I can in the main say nothing. But what one man, not entirely unfamiliar with such scenes before, *could* see, passing over the ground before, during, and after the fight, I saw; for the rest I must trust to such credible statements by the actors as I have been able to collect.

The Battle-Field

Whoever would carry in his mind a simple map of our positions in the great battles of Thursday and Friday, the second and third, at Gettysburg, has but to conceive a broad capital A, bisected by another line drawn down from the top and equi-distant from each side. These three straight lines meeting at the top of the letter are the three roads along which our army advanced, and between and on which lay the battlefield. The junction of the lines is Gettysburg. The middle line, running nearly north and south, is the road to Taneytown. The right-hand line, running southeast, is the Baltimore pike. That on the left is the Emmetsburg road.

Almost at the junction of the lines, and resting on the left-hand side of the Baltimore pike, is the key to the whole position—Cemetery Hill. This constitutes our extreme front, lies just south of Gettysburg, overlooks and completely commands the town; the entire valley to right and left, the whole space over which the rebels advanced to attack our centre, and a portion of the woods from which the rebel lines on their centre debouched.

Standing on this hill and facing north (toward the town) you have, just across the Baltimore pike, another hill, almost as high, and crowned like the Cemetery with batteries that rake the centre front. Farther to the right and rear, the country is broken into a series of short, billowy ridges, every summit of which affords a location for a battery. Through these passes the little valley of Rock Creek, crossing the Baltimore turnpike a couple of miles or so from town, and thus affording a good covered way for a rebel movement to attempt (by passing down the valley from the woods beyond this range of hills) to pierce our right wing, and penetrate to the rear of our centre.

On the left the hills are lower, afford fewer eligible positions for batteries, and are commanded by the heights on the rebel side.

The space between these lines is rolling, and in parts quite hilly; partially under cultivation, the rest lightly timbered; passable nearly everywhere for infantry and cavalry, in most parts for artillery also.

Our Line of Battle

The reader can now in an instant trace for himself our line of battle on the bisected A. Near the apex, the Cemetery, of course; batteries around the crest; infantry in line of battle down the declivity, in the orchard, and sweeping over the Taneytown road and up to that to Emmetsburg. Then along the stone fence which skirts the hither side of the Emmetsburg road for say half a mile. Then, bending in from the road a little, leaving its possession to our skirmishers alone, and so passing back for a mile and a half farther, in a line growing more and more distant from the Emmetsburg road, and nearer that to Taneytown. These are the lines of centre and left. Beginning at the Cemetery again, our right stretches *across* the Baltimore pike and along the range of hills already described, in a direction that grows nearly parallel with the pike, (at a distance from it of a quarter to half a mile,) and down it a couple of miles. Measuring all its sinuosities, the line must be about five miles long.

The Rebel Lines and Order of Battle

All the country fronting this remarkable horseshoe line is virtually in the hands of the rebels. It will be seen that their lines must be longer than ours, and that in moving from one point to another of the field they are compelled to make long detours, while our troops can be thrown from left to right, or from either to centre, with the utmost ease and by the shortest routes.

Take the crescent of the new moon, elongate the horns a little, turn the hollow side toward our positions, and you have the general direction the rebels were compelled to give their line of battle. As was seen in Wednesday's fight, Jackson's old corps under Ewell formed their left— opposite our right; while A. P. Hill held their centre, and Longstreet, who arrived early Thursday morning, their right.

Our Order of Battle

On our front the line of battle was arranged by General Meade, at an early hour on Thursday morning, as follows:

On the centre, holding Cemetery Hill and the declivity in its front, Major General Howard with his Eleventh corps. Across the pike on the adjacent hill to the right, what was left of the First corps. Next to it, and stretching to our extreme right, Major General Henry W. Slocum with his Twelfth corps. Beginning again at the Cemetery Hill, and going toward the left, we have first, next to Howard, the Second corps, Major General Hancock; next to it, the Third, Major General Daniel E. Sickles; and partly to the rear of the Third, and subsequently brought up on the extreme left, the Fifth corps, Major General George Sykes. The Sixth corps, Major General John Sedgwick, was kept near the Taneytown pike in the rear, and constituted the only reserve of the army.

Corps and Division Commanders

General readers are scarcely likely to be interested in minute details of the organization of the army, but perhaps it will be convenient to have a roster by corps and divisions, at least.

First Corps—Major General John F. Reynolds.

After General Reynold's death, General John Newton was assigned by General Meade to the command of this corps.

First Division . . . . Brigadier General James S. Wadsworth.
Second Division . . . . . . .Major General Abner Doubleday.
Third Division . . . . . Brigadier General John C. Robinson.

Second Corps—Major General Winfield S. Hancock.

First Division .... Brigadier General John C. Caldwell.
Second Division .... Brigadier General John Gibbon.
Third Division .... Brigadier General Alexander Hays.

Third Corps—Major General Daniel E. Sickles.

First Division .... Brigadier General John H. H. Ward.
Second Division .... Brigadier General Andrew A.
                                                    Humphreys.

Fifth Corps, (lately Meade's,) Major General George Sykes.

First Division .... Brigadier General James Barnes.
Second Division .... General Sykes*

Eleventh Corps—Major General Oliver O. Howard.

First Division .... Major General Carl Schurz.
Second Division .Brigadier General Adolph von Steinwehr.
Third Division ..... Brigadier General Francis C. Barlow.

Twelfth Corps—Major General Henry W. Slocum.

First Division .... Brigadier General John W. Geary.
Second Division ..... Brigadier General George S. Greene.
Third Division ... Brigadier General Alpheus S. Williams.*

* A number of errors appear in this listing. In the First Corps Robinson, in fact, commanded the Second Division and Doubleday the Third. In the Fifth Corps Brigadier General Romeyn B. Ayres commanded the Second Division. In the Eleventh Corps Barlow commanded the First Division and Schurz the Third. In the Twelfth Corps Williams commanded the First Division, Geary the Second, and Greene the Third Brigade in the Second Division.

Of John Sedgwick's splendid Sixth corps, which only became engaged as reserves, were brought in on Friday, I cannot give the division commanders now, (there have been such changes since Fredericksburg,) with any assurance of accuracy.

Our Concentration at Gettysburg

Our troops were not concentrated so early as those of the rebels, and but for their caution in so long feeling about our lines before making an attack, we might have suffered in consequence. Sedgwick's corps did not all get up till nearly dark Thursday evening, having been sent away beyond Westminster with a view to the intended movement on York. The Twelfth corps had arrived about sunset, Wednesday evening, a couple of hours or more after our repulse beyond Gettysburg; the Second and Third during that night, and the Fifth about ten Thursday morning. For Thursday's fight the Fifth constituted the only reserve.

Thursday till Four O'clock

All Thursday forenoon there was lively firing between our skirmishers and those of the enemy, but nothing betokening a general engagement. Standing on Cemetery Hill, which, but for its exposed position, constituted the best point of observation on the field, I could see the long line of our skirmishers stretching around centre and left, well advanced, lying flat on the ground in the meadows or cornfields and firing at will as they lay. The little streak of curling smoke that rose from their guns faded away in a

thin vapor that marked the course of the lines down the
left. With a glass the rebel line could be even more distinctly seen, every man of them with his blanket strapped
over his shoulder—no foolish "stripping for the fight" with
these trained soldiers. Occasionally the gray-coated fellows
rose from cover, and with a yell rushed on our men, firing
as they came. Once or twice in the half-hour that I
watched them, they did this with such impetuosity as to
force our skirmishers back, and call out a shell or two from
our nearest batteries—probably the very object their officers had in view.

Toward noon I rode over to general headquarters,
which had been established in a little, square, one-story,
whitewashed frame house, to the left and rear of the
cemetery, and just under the low hill where our left joined
the center. No part of the line was visible from the spot,
and it had been chosen, I suppose, because while within a
three minutes' gallop of the Cemetery, or the hither portion of the left, it seemed comparatively protected by its
situation. The choice was a bad one. Next to the Cemetery, it proved the hottest point on the field.

General Meade had finished his arrangement of the
lines. Reports of the skirmishing were coming in; the facts
developed by certain reconnoissances were being presented; the trim, well tailored person of Major General
Alfred Pleasanton was constantly passing in and out; the
cavalry seemed to be in incessant demand. General Williams and Major Simon F. Barstow, the Adjutant Generals,
were hard at work sending out the orders; aids and orderlies were galloping off and back; General G. K. Warren,
Acting Chief of Staff, was with the General Commanding,
poring over the maps of the field which the engineers had

just finished; most of the staff were stretched beneath an apple tree, resting while they could.

It seemed that a heavy pressure had been brought to bear for an attack on the enemy by the heads of columns in divisions, pouring the whole army on the enemy's centre, and smashing through it after the old Napoleonic plan; but Meade steadily resisted. The enemy was to fight him where he stood, was to come under the range of this long chain of batteries on the crests. Wisely decided, as the event proved.

The afternoon passed on in calm and cloudless splendor. From headquarters I rode down the left, then back to Slocum's headquarters on a high hill, half or three quarters of a mile south from the Cemetery, on the Baltimore pike. Everywhere quiet, the men stretched lazily on the ground in line of battle, horses attached to the caissons, batteries unlimbered and gunners resting on their guns.

The thunderbolts were shut up, like Æolus' winds; it seemed as if the sun might set in peace over all this mighty enginery of destruction held in calm, magnificent reserve.

The Rebel Attack on the Left

But unseen hands were letting loose the elements. General Meade had not failed to see the comparatively exposed position of our left; and between three and four the order was sent out for the extreme left—then formed by Sickle's (Third) corps—to advance. If the enemy was preparing to attack us there, our advance would soon unmask his movements.

It did. The corps moved out, spiritedly, of course—when even in disastrous days did it go otherwise to battle?—and by four o'clock had found the rebel advance. Longstreet was bringing up his whole corps—nearly a third of the rebel army—to precipitate upon our extreme left. The fight at once opened with artillery first, presently with crashing roars of musketry, too. Rebel batteries were already in position, and some of them enfiladed Sickle's line. Our own were hastily set to work, and the most dangerous of the rebel guns were partially silenced. Then came a rebel charge with the wild yell and rush; it is met by a storm of grape and canister from our guns depressed to rake them in easy range. The line is shattered and sent whirling back on the instant. Long columns almost immediately afterward begin to debouch from the woods to the rear of the rebel batteries—another and a grander charge is preparing. General Warren who, as Chief of Staff, is overlooking the fight for the Commanding General, sends back for more troops. Alas! Sedgwick's corps is not yet available. We have only the Fifth for the reserves. Howard and Hancock are already at work on the centre and left centre. But Hancock advances, and the fire grows intenser still along the whole line of the left.

Meantime, Cemetery Hill is raked at once from front and left, and the shells from rebel batteries on the left carry over even into the positions held by our right. The battle rages on but one side, but death moves visibly over the whole field from line to line and front to rear. Trains are hurried away on the Baltimore pike; the unemployed *debris* of the army takes alarm, a panic in the rear seems impending. Guards thrown hastily across the roads to send the runaways back, do something to repress it.

The rebel lines we have seen debouching behind their batteries on Sickle's front slowly advance. The fight grows desperate, aid after aid is sent for reinforcements; our front wavers, the line of flame and smoke sways to and fro, but slowly settles backward. Sickles is being—not driven—but pushed back. At last the reserve comes in; the advance of the brigades of the Fifth wind down among the rocks and enter the smoke, the line braces up, advances, halts soon, but comes no more back. The left is not overpowered yet. We had had two hours of exceedingly severe artillery and musketry fighting. The enemy still holds a little of the ground we had, but the chances seem almost even.

One Phase—A Type of Many

I cannot trace the movements further in detail; let me give one phase of the fight, fit type of many more. Some Massachusetts batteries—Captain John Bigelow's, Captain Charles A. Phillip's, two or three more under Captain Freeman McGilvery of Maine—were planted on the extreme left, advanced now well down to the Emmetsburg road, with infantry in their front—the first division, I think, of Sickle's corps. A little after five a fierce rebel charge drove back the infantry and menaced the batteries. Orders are sent to Bigelow on the extreme left, to hold his position at every hazard short of sheer annihilation, till a couple more batteries can be brought to his support. Reserving his fire a little, then with depressed guns opening with double charges of grape and canister, he smites and shatters, but cannot break the advancing line. His grape and canister are exhausted, and still, closing grandly up over their slain, on they come. He falls back on spherical case, and pours this in at the shortest range. On, still onward comes the artillery-defying line, and still he holds his position. They are within six paces of the guns—he fires again. Once more, and he blows devoted soldiers from his very muzzles. And still mindful of that solemn order, he holds his place. They spring upon his carriages and shoot down his horses! And then, his Yankee artillerists still about him, he seizes the guns by hand, and from the very front of that line drags two of them off. The caissons are further back—five out of the six are saved.

That single company, in that half-hour's fight, lost thirty-three of its men, including every sergeant it had. The Captain himself was wounded. Yet it was the first time it was ever under fire! I give it simply as a type. *So* they fought along that fiery line!

The rebels now poured on Phillips's battery, and it, too, was forced to drag off the pieces by hand when the horses were shot down. From a new position it opened again; and at last the two reinforcing batteries came up on the gallop. An enfilading fire swept the rebel line; Sickle's gallant infantry charged, the rebel line swept back on a refluent tide—we regained the lost ground, and every gun just lost in this splendid fight.

Once more I repeat, this is but a type.

Reinforcements Called in from the Right

Slocum, too, came into the fight. The reserves were all used up; the right seemed safe. It was believed from the terrific attack that the whole rebel army, Ewell's corps included, was massed on our centre and left; and so a single brigade was left to hold the rifle-pits constructed through the day along the whole line of the Twelfth on the right; and the rest of the corps came across the little neck of land to strengthen our weakening line. Needful, perhaps, but perilous in the extreme.

The Close

At six the cannonade grew fiercer than ever, and the storm of death swept over the field from then till darkness ended the conflict. In the main our strengthened columns held the line. At points they were forced back a little; a few prisoners were lost. On the whole the rebels were unsuccessful, but we had not quite held our own.

Some caissons had been blown up on either side; a barn on the Emmetsburg road was fired by the rebel shells, and its light gave their sharpshooters a little longer time at that point to work. Both sides lay on their arms exhausted, but insatiate, to wait for the dawning.

Results and Doubtful Issue

The Third and Second corps were badly shattered. The Eleventh had not been quite so much engaged—its artillery had kept the rebels at a greater distance—but it had behaved well. Sickles was wounded—a leg shot off; General Samuel K. Zook was killed; our own old townsman Colonel Edward E. Cross was killed; the farm houses and barns for miles were filled with the wounded. The rebels had left us William Barksdale, dying; what other losses they had met we could only conjecture from the piles of dead the last rays of the sun had shown along their front.

And so, with doubtful prospects, darkness came like a wall between us, and compelled nature's truce.

From the right there came sudden, sharp volleys of cheers; Ewell had *not* gone; a hasty rush had carried some of Slocum's rifle-pits, protected only by the long drawn out line of a single brigade. It was a gloomy close. That was our strongest point, where Jackson's men had gained their fortified foothold.

Now, indeed, if ever, may the nation well wrestle with God in prayer. We have fought but three hours and a half; have lost on both flanks; have called every reserve we had on the field into action, and with daybreak must hold these shattered columns to the work again. Well may the land take up the refrain of George Henry Boker's touching hymn for the Philadelphia Fourth.

> "Help us, Lord, our only trust!
> We are helpless, we are dust!
> All our homes are red with blood;
> Long our grief we have withstood;
> Every lintel, each door post,
> Drips, at tidings from the host,
> With the blood of some one lost.
> Help us, Lord, our only trust!
> We are helpless, we are dust!"

The Opening—Friday Morning

I must be pardoned some egotism in what remains. It is easiest to narrate what one has seen, and undue prominence may thus come to be given to certain points, for time and space press me more and more.

At day break crashing volleys woke the few sleepers there were. A fusilade ran along the line—each had felt the other, then came cautious skirmishing again.

But on the right there was no cessation. Ewell's men were in possession of part of our riflepits, and sought to gain the remainder; Slocum must defend the one part and regain the other at every hazard. They were fighting Stonewall Jackson's men—it might well be desperate work.

I had gone down the Baltimore pike at night to find a resting-place—coming up between four and five, I heard clearly on the right the old charging cheer. Once, twice, three times I counted it, as my horse pushed his way for less than a mile through the curious or coward throng that ebbed and flowed along the pike. Each time a charge was made, each time the musketry fire leaped out from our line more terrific than before, and still the ground was held. To the left and centre, firing gradually ceased. All interest was concentrated on this fierce contest on the right; the rest of the line on either side was bracing itself for still more desperate work.

From four to five there was heavy cannonading also, from our batteries nearest the contested points, but the artillery fire diminished and presently ceased. The rebels made no reply; we were firing at random, and it was a useless waste of ammunition. A cloud of smoke curled up from the dark woods on the right; the musketry crash continued with unparalleled tenacity and vehemence, wounded men came back over the fields, a few stragglers were hurried out to the front, ammunition was kept conveniently near the line.

In the fields to the left of the Baltimore pike stood the reserve artillery, with horses harnessed to the pieces and ready to move on the instant. Cavalry, too, was drawn up in detachments here and there. Moved over already within

supporting distance of Slocum's line stood a part of Sedgwick's corps, (the reserve of today,) ready for the emergency that seemed likely soon to demand it. Occasional
bullets from the rebel front spattered against the trees and
fences. Now and then a Minie went over with its buzzing
hiss, but the pike was too nearly out of range to be cleared
of the watching throng.

General Sickles

Through this throng with slow tread there came a file
of soldiers, armed, but marching to the rear. It was a guard
of honor for one who well deserved it. On a stretcher,
borne by a couple of stout privates, lay General Sickles—
but yesterday leading his corps with all the enthusiasm and
dash for which he has been distinguished—today with his
right leg amputated, and lying there, grim and stoical, with
his cap pulled over his eyes, his hands calmly folded across
his breast, and *a cigar in his mouth!* For a man who had
just lost a leg, and whose life was yet in imminent jeopar-
dy, it was cool indeed. He was being taken to the nearest
railroad line, to be carried to some city where he could get
most careful attendance; and the guard that accompanied
him showed that already there was some apprehensions for
the rear.

There was reason for it. Less than an hour later orders
were issued from Pleasanton's headquarters, a mile or so
further back on the Baltimore pike, for Colonel J. Irvin
Gregg to take his cavalry force and guard against a dash
down the valley of Rock Creek into the rear and centre.
The rebels met the preparation and drew back to try it
soon again further out the line.

The Battle on the Right

I rode up the high hill where General Slocum's headquarters were established; but though it afforded an excel-
lent view of most of our positions, the fight going on was
concealed by a mask of woods on the distant hills. The
Rodman guns on the hill were all manned, and the gunners
were eager to try their range, but it still seemed useless.
Firing in the woods, they were as likely to hit friend as
foe. Signal officers here were in communication with general headquarters, with Howard on Cemetery Hill, Hancock next [to] him on the right, and one or two of the headquarters on the left. There was no fear of lack of certain
communication between the different portions of the field,
let the fortunes of the day go what way they would.

As I rode down the slope and up through the wheat
fields to Cemetery Hill, the batteries began to open again
on points along our outer line. They were evidently playing on what had been Slocum's line of yesterday. The
rebels, then, were there still, in our rifle pits. Presently the
battery on Slocum's hill gained the long-sought permission,
and opened, too, aiming apparently in the same direction.
Other batteries along the inner line, just to the left of the
Baltimore pike, followed the signal, and as one after another opened up, till every little crest between Slocum's
headquarters and Cemetery Hill began belching its thunder, I had to change my course through the wheat fields to
avoid our own shells.

Still no artillery response from the rebels. Could they be
short of ammunition? Could they have failed to bring up
all their guns? Were they, perhaps, massing artillery else-
where, and only keeping up this furious crash of musketry
on the right as a blind?

By eight o'clock I had reached Cemetery Hill. Yesterday's conflict was more plainly inscribed on the tombstones than the virtues of the buried dead they commemorated. Shells had plouged up lately sodded graves; round shot had shattered marble columns; dead horses lay about among the monuments, and the gore of dead men soaked the soil and moistened the roots of flowers on the old graves.

This morning it was comparatively quiet again. Sharpshooters from the houses in the town were picking off officers who exposed themselves along the crest. They knew that we did not want to shell the place, and presumed upon the forebearance of our artillery. The annoyance had at last become too serious, and one of our guns had been directed to dislodge a nest of the most audacious and the surest aimed by battering down the house from which they were firing. It was the only house in Gettysburg we harmed throughout the battles.

To the front skirmishers were still at work, but in a desultory way. All eyes were turned to the right; where now that our artillery had taken its share in the contest, its intensity seemed but redoubled by Ewell's men. Distinctly, even amid all this roar, there came up the sound of another of those ominous cheers; and the hurricane of crashing sound that followed seemed tearing the forest trees and solid hillside asunder. It was another rebel charge. Standing by the gatekeeper's lodge, with a glass I could distinctly see our shattered line swinging irregularly and convulsively back from those death-bearing woods. The rebel yells redoubled, but so did our artillery fire, now that the gunners saw exactly where to throw. The retreat lasted for but a moment, the line straightened, rallied, plunged into the woods again.

A Tried General

All this while—the fire gradually getting a little hotter on the hill, and an occasional shell from the rebel guns, now beginning to open, coming over—General Howard was calmly reclining against a hillock by a grave stone, with his staff about him. One or two he kept constantly watching the right, and occasionally sweeping the whole rebel line with their glasses; the rest were around him, ready for instant service. I have seen many men in action, but never so imperturbably cool as this General of the Eleventh corps. I watched him closely as a Minie whizzed overhead. *I* dodged, of course; I never expect to get over that habit; but I am confident he did not move a muscle by the fraction of a hair's breadth.

Progress on the Right

About a quarter after nine the conflict in the woods to the right seemed to be culminating. Clouds of smoke obscured the view, but beyond that smoke we knew that our noble line the Twelfth and a part of the First with some reserves were now engaged was holding its ground; the direction of the sound even seemed to indicate that it was gaining, but of course that was a very uncertain test. "Ride over to General Meade," said Howard to one of his aids, "and tell him the fighting on the right seems more terrific than ever and appears swinging somewhat toward the centre, but that we know little or nothing of how the battle goes, and ask him if he has any orders." In a few minutes the aid galloped back. "The troops are to stand to arms, sir, and watch the front."

Meantime there was a little diversion away down toward

the extreme right. A brigade had been thrown east of Rock Creek to watch the possible attempt at repeating the effort to get down the valley into our rear. Finding a good opportunity, it began to pour in its volleys upon Ewell's flank. The audacity of a single brigade attempting such a thing was beyond rebel suspicion; they naturally thought a heavy force was turning their flank, and were less inclined to push on Slocum's sorely pressed men in front.

Nothing seemed to come of Howard's "watching the front"; the fire of skirmishers revived occasionally and then died away again; and finally, about a quarter before ten, I started over to general headquarters. In descending the Cemetery Hill and crossing the intervening fields, I noticed that some bullets were beginning to come over from our left, but supposed them of course to be merely stray shots from the rebel skirmishers.

The Commander-in Chief at Headquarters

Headquarters presented a busy scene. Meade was receiving reports in the little house, coming occasionally to the door to address a hasty inquiry to some one in the group of staff officers under the tree. Quick and nervous in his movements, but calm, and as it seemed to me, lit up with the glow of the occasion, he looked more the General, less the student. Polished, fashionable looking Pleasanton, riding whip resting in the leg of one of his jackboots, and neatly fitting kids drawn over his hands, occasionally put in some earnest remark. Warren, calm, absorbed, earnest as ever, was constantly in consultation wtih the Commander.

In all matters of detail, Williams or Major Barstow was referred to as to an encylopedia. Orderlies and aids were momentarily dashing up with reports and off with orders; the signal officers were bringing in the reports telegraphed by the signal flags from the different crests that over-looked the fight. The rest of the staff stood ready for any duty, and outside the little garden fence a great group of horses stood hitched.

Headquarters Under Fire

Wilkeson, my original companion from Baltimore, was up at last and very sad. His son, a gallant young lieutenant of regular artillery, had had his leg shot off in Wednesday's disastrous fight, and whether living now or dead he could not tell; he was a prisoner (or a corpse) in Gettysburg.

We walked around to the east of the little house and lay down on the grass. Others were there; there was much comparison of views, talk of probabilities, gossip of the arrival of militia from Harrisburg. The fight still raged furiously on the right. Headquarters were under a slight fire. The balls from the left seemed to increase a little in number; a few came over from the front; we saw no damage that any of them did.

Close by our heads went one, evidently from some kind of small arm that had an unfamiliar sound. "That," said Wilkeson, aesthetic always or nothing, "that is a muffled howl; that's the exact phrase to describe it." We discussed the question.

Wh-r-sh-shh! A sudden exclamation and start all around the group. "Jove!" exclaims one, impulsively; "those fellows on the left have the range of headquarters exactly." It was a round shot that had passed not two feet from the door and buried itself in the road three or four yards in front of us. In an instant there was another and another. General Meade came to the door, told the staff that they manifestly had our range, and that they had best go up the slope fifteen or twenty yards to the stable. As they started, a couple of shells came, then more from a different direction, and a sharp fusilade broke out just behind us on the left. Two rebel batteries clearly had our range, and the fight seemed opening up on the field of last night's bitterest contest.

A few minutes before, I had been talking of going down to look at Barksdale's corpse—there was other work to do than looking at dead men now. Leaving the late headquarters to the shells, I galloped out the Taneytown road along the left. For three quarters of a mile the fire was bursting out.

The air was alive with all mysterious sounds, and death in every one of them. There were "muffled howls" that seemed in rage because their missile missed you, the angry buzz of the familiar Minie, the *spit* of the common musket ball, hisses, and the great whirring rushes of shells. And then there came others that made the air instinct with warning, or quickened it with vivid alarm; long wails that fatefully bemoaned the death they wrought; fluttering screams that filled the whole space with their horror, and encompassed one about as a garment; cries that ran the diapason of terror and despair.

Rise and Ebb of the Tide of Battle

It had been a sudden concentration of terrific artillery fire on our left, with a view to silence our batteries and sweep resistance from the slopes before they charged. But they did not find us unprepared. The tornado of death that swept over the fields levelled much before it, but not all. After an hour or two it was found that the obstinate defenders still clung to their positions; and the rebels saw they must reserve their energies for the more determined and persistent effort the afternoon was to bring. On it, as on the last toss of the dice, they had staked their all. In an hour or two the left was silent again; on the centre there was but the accustomed straggling shots.

The Right Victorious

Meantime on the right, the fierceness of Ewell's attack had dashed itself out, and but feeble surges came up now against our line. Leaving the left as the attack there was dying away, I rode over again to Slocum's Hill on the Baltimore pike. From this high eminence we could only make out that the line seemed in its old place, and so the officers said it was. The rifle pits had been regained; Ewell's corps had been substantially repulsed. The musketry still flickered sharply up occasionally, but the fire had gone out of it. We were practically victorious on the right. It was a quarter past eleven—seven hours and a quarter of desperate fighting! The old Jackson corps had not given up without an obstinate struggle.

Cavalry—A Lull

Away down from the extreme right, and apparently beyond it, there came a ripple of musketry. It was said to be William F. Smith's division from Major General Darius N. Couch's Harrisburg force, coming in on Ewell's flank or rear. I have not yet been able to satisfy myself whether the report was true or not.

A quarter of an hour later Pleasanton's scouts reported rebel cavalry coming in on the Bonaughtown road on the right to strike the Baltimore pike in our rear. Gregg was instantly sent off to meet them, with orders merely to hold them in check, and not to bring on a close engagement if he could avoid it. At the same time Brigadier General Judson Kilpatrick was ordered to the extreme left to harass the enemy's flank and rear and look after his trains. "Good!" exclaimed Kilpatrick, rubbing his hands, and in a moment was hurrying gleefully to execute the order.

Gregg threw his force up a little brook that comes down between Rock Creek and the post village of Two Taverns. The rebel cavalry no sooner saw their plan detected than they retired. But their effort was not over, and fortunately Gregg understood it. Under cover of the woods, they moved still further south, in a direction parallel with the Baltimore pike; but Gregg was moving too, and when they started out toward the pike, they were again confronted. There was a little carbine firing now, and some sharp shelling, and the rebels again retired. Once more they came out, almost opposite Two Taverns, late in the afternoon, but Gregg was still on the watch for them, and they at once and finally retired without a shot.

There was a lull from a quarter past eleven to about one. Fitful firing broke out and died away again here and there, but the lines were mainly silent. The rebels were not yet defeated—except for the hour's sharp work on the left, two of their corps with their reserves had not been engaged at all today. Some final desperate effort must be maturing.

Shrewd officers predicted that it would be a massing of all their troops on the left. But Ewell's corps could not possibly be brought over in time for that; its work for the day must be nearly done.

The Last Desperate Attack*

Pretty soon the attack came—sooner, indeed, and wider than was expected. About one the rebel movement was developed in a thunder of cannonading that rolled over our army like doom. They had concentrated immense quantities of artillery—"two hundred and fifty pieces, at least," some of General Meade's staff-officers said, on our centre and left, and those devoted lines were to bear the last, fiercest shock, that, staunchly met, should leave the exhausted rebel army drifting back from its supreme effort, a defeated host. Longstreet and A. P. Hill were to support and follow up the artillery attack, and the reserves were with them.

Soon, from the Cemetery hill, (I did not see this, but tell it as actors in it told me,) could be seen the forming columns of Hill's corps. Their batteries had already opened in almost a semicircle of fire on that scarred hill front. Three cross fires thus came in upon it, and today the tracks of shells ploughing the ground in as many directions may be seen everywhere among the graves. Howard never moved his headquarters an inch. There was his Eleventh corps, and there he meant to stay and make them do their duty if he could. They did it well.

* Pickett's Charge.

When the fierce cannonade had, as they supposed, sufficiently prepared the way, down came the rebel lines, "dressed to the right" as if for a parade before some grand master of reviews. To the front they had a line of skirmishers, double or treble the usual strength, next the line of battle for the charge, next another equally strong in reserve, if the fierce fire they might meet should melt away the first.

Howard sent orders for his men to lie down, and for a little our batteries ceased firing. The rebels thought they had silenced us and charged. They were well up to our front when that whole corps of concealed Germans sprang up and poured out their sheet of flame and smoke, and swiftly flying death; the batteries opened—the solid lines broke, and crisped up into little fragments, and were beaten widely back. Our men charged; company after company, once at least a whole regiment, threw down their arms and rushed over to be taken prisoners and carried out of this fearful fire.

Simultaneously, similar scenes were enacting along the front of the Second, Third, and Fifth corps. Everywhere the rebel attack was beaten back, and the cannonade on both sides continued at its highest pitch.

When this broke out, I had been coming over from the neighborhood of Pleasanton's headquarters. Ascending the high hill to the rear of Slocum's headquarters, I saw such a sight as few men ever hope to see twice in a lifetime. Around our centre and left, the rebel line must have been from four to five miles long, and over that whole length there rolled up the smoke from their two hundred and fifty guns. The roar, the bursting bombs, the impression of magnificient power, "all the glory visible, all the horror of the fearful field concealed," a nation's existence trembling as the clangor of those iron monsters swayed the balance—it was a sensation for a century!

About two the fire slackened a little, then broke out deadlier than ever, till, beaten out against our impenetrable sides, it ebbed away, and closed in broken, spasmodic dashes.

The great, desperate, final charge came at four. The rebels seemed to have gathered up all their strength and desperation for one fierce, convulsive effort, that should sweep over and wash out our obstinate resistance. They swept up as before, the flower of their army to the front, victory staked upon the issue. In some places they literally lifted up and pushed back our lines, but, that terrible "position" of ours!—wherever they entered it, enfilading fires from half a score of crests swept away their columns like merest chaff. Broken and hurled back, they easily fell into our hands, and on the centre and left the last half-hour brought more prisoners than all the rest.

So it was along the whole line; but it was on the Second corps that the flower of the rebel army was concentrated; it was there that the heaviest shock beat upon and shook and even sometimes crumbled our line.

We had some shallow rifle pits, with barricades of rails from the fences. The rebel line, stretching away miles to the left, in magnificent array, but strongest here—Pickett's splendid division of Longstreet's corps in front, the best of A. P. Hill's veterans in support—came steadily and as it seemed resistlessly sweeping up. Our skirmishers retired slowly from the Emmetsburg road, holding their ground tenaciously to the last. The rebels reserved their fire till they reached this same Emmetsburg road, then opened with a terrific crash. From a hundred iron throats, meantime, their artillery had been thundering on our barricades.

Hancock was wounded; Gibbon succeeded to the command—a proved soldier and ready for the crisis. As the tempest of fire approached its height, he walked along the line and renewed his orders to the men to reserve their fire. The rebels—three lines deep—came steadily up. They were in point blank range.

At last the order came! From thrice six thousand guns there came a sheet of smoky flame, a crash, a rush of leaden death. The line literally melted away; but there came a second, resistless still. It had been our supreme effort—on the instant we were not equal to another.

Up to the rifle pits, across them, over the barricades— the momentum of their charge, the mere machine strength of their combined action swept them on. Our thin line could fight, but it had not weight enough to oppose to this momentum. It was pushed behind the guns. Right on came the rebels. They were upon the guns, were bayoneting the gunners, were waving their flags above our pieces.

But they had penetrated to the fatal point. A storm of grape and canister tore its way from man to man and marked its track with corpses straight down their line! They had exposed themselves to the enfilading fire of the guns on the western slope of Cemetery Hill; that exposure sealed their fate.

The line reeled back—disjointed already—in an instant in fragments. Our men were just behind the guns. They leaped forward upon the disordered mass; but there was little need for fighting now. A regiment threw down its arms, and with colors at its head rushed over and surrendered. All along the field small detachments did the same. Webb's brigade brought in eight hundred taken in as little time as it requires to write the simple sentence that tells it. Gibbon's old division took fifteen stand of colors.

Over the fields the escaped fragments of the charging line fell back—the battle there was over. A single brigade, Brigadier General William Harrow's, (of which the Seventh Michigan is part,) came out with fifty-four less officers, seven hundred and ninety-three less men than it took in! So the whole corps fought—so too they fought further down the line.

Finis

It was fruitless sacrifice. They gathered up their broken fragments, formed their lines, and slowly marched away. It was not a rout, it *was* a bitter crushing defeat. For once the Army of the Potomac had won a clean, honest, acknowledged victory.

Yet we were very near defeat. Our ammunition had grown scant; the reserve ammunition train had been brought up and drained; but for that we should have been left to cold steel.

Brigade after brigade had been thrown forward to strengthen the line; as the rebel attack drifted back over the fields there stood in the rear just one single brigade that constituted the entire reserve of the Army of the Potomac. Forty thousand fresh troops to have hurled forward upon that retreating mass would have ended the campaign with the battle; but, for forty thousand we had that one wasted brigade! The rebels were soon formed again, and ready for defence—the opportunity was lost!

Shells still dropped over the Cemetery, by the headquarters and in the wheat fields toward the Baltimore pike; but the fight was over.

Headquarters were established anew under the trees in a little wood near Slocum's Hill. General Meade rode up, calm as ever, and called for paper and aids; he had orders already to issue. A band came marching in over the hillside; on the evening air its notes floated out—significant melody—"Hail to the Chief."

"Ah! General Meade," said W., "you're in very great danger of being President of the United States." "No," said another, more wisely, as it seems. "Finish well this work so well begun, and the position you have is better and prouder than President."

After the Battle

Our campaign "after the invaders" was over. There was brief time for last glances at the field, last questions after the dead and dying—then the hurried trip west, and the misery of putting together, from the copious notes taken on the field, on swaying railroad cars, and amid jostly crowds, the story of the day.

The morning after the battle was as sweet and fresh as though no storm of death had all the day before been sweeping over those quiet Pennsylvania hills and valleys. The roads were lined with ambulances, returning to the field for the last of the wounded; soldiers exchanging greetings after the battle with their comrades and comparing notes of the day; officers looking after their wounded men or hunting up the supplies for their regiments. Detachments of rebel prisoners every few moments passed back under guard; the woods inside our line had been full of them all night, and we were just beginning to gather them up. Everybody was in the most exuberant spirits. For once this army had won a real victory—the soldiers felt it, and the sensation was so novel, they could not but be ecstatic.

The Field

Along the lines on the left a sharp popping of skirmishers was still kept up. I rode down over the scene of yesterday's fiercest conflict, and at the cost of some exposure, and the close passage of a couple of Minie balls, got a view of the thickly strewn rebel corpses that still cast up to heaven their mute protest against the treason that had made them what they were. But the details of these horrible scenes are too sickening, and alas! too familiar; I must be excused from their description.

At Headquarters

Headquarters—still over in the woods near Slocum's Hill—were in bivouac. The General had a little wall tent, in which he was dictating orders and receiving despatches; General Ingalls, the Chief Quartermaster, had his writing table in the open of a covered wagon; the rest, majors, colonels, generals and all, had slept on the ground, and were now standing about the campfires, hands full of fried pork and hard bread, making their breakfasts in a style that a year ago would have astonished the humblest private in the Army of the Potomac.

The cavalry generals were again in request, and heavy reconnoissances were ordered. The bulk of the rebel army was believed to be in full retreat; one strong corps could still be seen, strongly posted on well chosen heights to the northward and drawn up in line of battle to repel any attempt at direct pursuit.

The casualties on the staff were wonderfully small. General Warren, acting Chief of Staff, had a remarkable escape. A Minie ball passed directly under his chin, cut his throat in a little line that, with half an inch's motion in his head, or change in the direction of the ball, would have been converted into a deathly wound. As it was, his shirt was stained with the blood that trickled down, but he did not think the wound worth binding up.

It has been telegraphed and re-telegraphed and telegraphed again from headquarters, that General Butterfield was badly wounded. He received a slight blow on the back Friday afternoon from a spent fragment of shell, I believe; but it did not even break the skin.

These, with the wounding of Lieutenant Colonel Joseph Dickinson, Aid to General Meade, constituted the only casualties on the staff.

Major Barstow, the efficient Adjutant-General, received fragments of shells on both sides of his saddle but escaped unhurt.

The Fire at Headquarters

It was not, however, because they had little exposure that their losses were small. How we were nearly all driven away from headquarters Friday forenoon by the furious cannonade has already been told; but my friend and companion on that morning, Mr. Samuel Wilkeson of the New York *Times,* has so vividly described the scene that I must be allowed to reproduce it:

"In the shadow cast by the tiny farm house, sixteen by twenty, which General Meade had made his headquarters, lay wearied staff officers and tired correspondents. There was not wanting to the peacefulness of the scene the singing of a bird, which had a nest in a peach tree within the tiny yard of the white washed cottage. In the midst of its warbling, a shell screamed over the house, instantly followed by another and another, and in a moment the air was full of the most complete artillery prelude to an infantry battle that was ever exhibited. Every size and form of shell known to British and to American gunnery, shrieked, whirled, moaned, and whistled and wrathfully fluttered over our ground. As many as six in a second, constantly two in a second, bursting and screaming over and around the headquarters, made a very hell of fire that amazed the oldest officers. They burst in the yard—burst next to the fence on both sides, garnished as usual with the hitched horses of aides and orderlies. The fastened animals reared and plunged with terror. Then one fell, then another—sixteen lay dead and mangled before the fire ceased, still fastened by their halters, which gave the expression of being wickedly tied up to die painfully. These brute victims of a cruel war touched all hearts. Through the midst of the storm of screaming and exploding shells, an ambulance driven by its frenzied conductor at full speed, presented to all of us the marvellous spectacle of a horse going rapidly on three legs. A hinder one had been shot off at the hock. A shell tore up the little step at the headquarters cottage, and ripped bags of oats as with a knife. Another soon carried off one of its two pillars. Soon a spherical case burst opposite the open door—another ripped through the low garret. The remaining pillar went almost immediately to the howl of a fixed shot that Whitworth must have made. During this fire the horses at twenty and thirty feet distant were receiving their death, and soldiers in Federal blue were torn to pieces in the road, and died with the peculiar yells that blend the extorted cry of pain with horror and despair. Not an orderly—not an ambulance—not a straggler was to be seen upon the plain swept by this tempest of orchestral death, thirty minutes after it commenced. Were not one hundred and twenty pieces of artillery trying to cut from the field every battery we had in position to resist their purposed infantry attack, and to sweep away the slight defences behind which our infantry were waiting? Forty minutes—fifty minutes—counted watches that ran, oh! so languidly! Shells through the two lower rooms. A shell into the chimney, that daringly did not explode. Shells in the yard. The air thicker and fuller and more deafening with the howling and whirring of these infernal missiles. The Chief of Staff struck—Seth Williams— loved and respected through the army, separated from instant death by two inches of space vertically measured. An aid bored with a fragment of iron through the bone of the arm. And the time measured on the sluggish watches was one hour and forty minutes."

How the Correspondents Faced Death

To this vivid description, in justice to its author, let me add that Mr. Wilkeson stayed at the house during the whole terrible cannonade. Mr. Frank Henry, also of the *Times*, likewise stood it out. Their accounts may well be said to have the smell of fire upon them!

C. C. Coffin, of the Boston *Journal*, and L. L. Crounse, of the New York *Times* as well as several other journalists of whom I knew less, were at different times under almost equally heavy fire. Mr. Crounse had his horse shot under him during Thursday's engagement. Such perils are they compelled to face who would be able to say something more of a battle than what those who are first out of it, can tell.

Once More on Cemetery Hill—Departure

We could linger no longer on the field. My companion for the last day or two, Mr. Coffin, and myself, resolved on reaching Baltimore that night. The Northern Central Railroad was still broken, and from Baltimore my shortest road west lay *via* Philadelphia. With such a circuitous route ahead, there was no time to spare.

We rode up the Cemetery hill for a last look at the field. It was ploughed and torn in every direction by the fierce crossfires of artillery that had spent their force upon it. Dead men, decently laid out, were in the gate keeper's lodge. Upturned, swollen horses lay among the tombs, where the sudden shot or shell had stricken them down. Batteries still frowned from the crest; away to the front of the rebel line (a strong rearguard only now) could still be distinctly seen. Howard, Carl Schurz, Steinwehr, and two or three others of lesser rank, were watching the movements through their glasses and discussing the probabilities.

There was a rush of letters to be mailed and telegraph messages to be sent. Among the number came Henry Ward Beecher's son, a bluff hearty looking youth. He had a despatch to Mrs. Stowe he wanted me to send, announcing that her son, too, was among the wounded and would soon be sent home to her.

On an old grave that a shell had rudely torn, while a

round shot had battered down the iron railing about it, were still blooming the flowers affection's hand had planted in more peaceful times—not a petal shaken off by all this tempest that had swept and whirled and torn about them. Human blood watered the roots—patriot blood that made them doubly sacred. I stooped and gathered them—roses and columbine and modest, sweet-scented pinks, mingled with sprigs of cypress—they are my only trophy from that glorious field.

Good-by to Gettysburg—a mad gallop to Westminster, (which brought our day's ride up to nearly fifty miles,) to catch a train that after all, loaded with wounded soldiers as it was, spent the whole night backing and hauling on side tracks and switches; and so at last to Baltimore; and out of the field once more. May it be forever.

Effect of Lee's Escape

1863, July 17

"This puts us back into next year." Such was Vice President Hamilin's exclamation as the escape of Lee's army was announced to him. That was in the midst of our forces and under all the influences that always exist there favorable to delay and apologetic for disaster. Here the feeling seems to have been at once more decided and more bitter. The President declares Lee's escape the greatest blunder of the war. Others are not wanting to cry already for some man who can pursue and fight.

Justice to a man who needs all he can get of it requires me to add that, in persistency of urging action at least, General Halleck was not this time to blame. Whether he was equally energetic in furnishing and directing aright the means of action is another question. General Meade telegraphed him that there was a difference in his Council of War, and that he was hesitating about making an attack. Halleck replied: "It is proverbial that Councils of War never fight, attack the enemy at once, and hold Councils of War afterward." The order was good; but, by the time it arrived, the enemy had escaped by a pontoon bridge, which Halleck had not prevented from being sent up the south side of the Potomac.

Today it is rumored that Meade has asked to be relieved of command. It is certain that the old swarm of personal imbroglios in the Army of the Potomac has broken out again. Meantime we have crossed the river, but the indications do not foreshadow a very vigorous pursuit.

VII

The Struggle for the Negro

Reid's answer, like that of many Americans, to the race problem of the 1850's was colonization. The possibility of successful secession, however, as well as the impracticality of colonization led him to endorse full citizenship for the Negro in the 1860's. The years of War and Reconstruction marked Reid's most liberal attitudes toward the black race. The sections that follow show his endorsement to be, if not of the crusading kind, at least forthright and forceful.

General Hunter's Negro Soldiers

1862, July 6

Gen. David Hunter's letter about his Negro soldiers brought up a lively debate in the House Saturday, in which some very conservative men said some very ultra things, that must prove sadly 'firing for the Southern heart. Charles A. Wickliffe [Whig, Ky.] wanted to reconsider the vote by which Hunter's letter was ordered printed and couldn't contain himself on the insult Hunter had offered to local people. He charged officers of the Government and of the army with having undertaken without law, against order, and in violation of every principle of hu-

71

manity, to assume the power of enlisting slaves to serve against their masters. General Hunter's letter was in manner and terms unbecoming a General. He held Secretary Stanton responsible for Hunter's conduct and sneeringly said Hunter had better been seeing to his business when the late disaster in South Carolina took place than tinkering with Negroes. Robert Mallory [Dem., Ky.] made the usual Kentucky speech against arming the blacks. He ridiculed the idea of making them soldiers; said a single cannon shot would put ten thousand of them to flight; and closed by declaring that arming them was barbarous, inhuman and contrary to the practice of all civilized nations, and that it was most as bad as putting the tomahawk into the hands of the savage. This stirred up Thaddeus Stevens, who inquired, how does it come that they are so dangerous to their masters, when a single cannon shot will put ten thousand to flight? Or how is it they have not courage enough to make soldiers when you call them as savage and dangerous as Indians? But the gentleman was mistaken in his facts. Common history, he repeated, proved them false. It had been the general practise of civilized nations to employ slaves for military purposes, whenever and wherever needed. Owen Lovejoy [Rep., Ill.] here begged leave to interrupt, and read from common school history about Jackson's arming slaves in the War of 1812 and his promise to give freedom to all who served. He then read Jackson's General Order, thanking the Negroes for their gallant success, saying that he had not been unaware of their good qualities as soldiers, but that they had far surpassed his highest expectations and reassuring them of emancipation as a reward for their conduct. Lovejoy concluded his demonstration on the Negro-frightened gentlemen by reference to another history, showing that one fourth of the men who helped with Perry's victory on the lakes were Negroes. The effect of all this was sensational. Men who had been denouncing Hunter couldn't have been more astonished if one of Hunter's own bombshells from Port Royal had been dropped among them.

Charles B. Sedgewick [Rep., N.Y.] heightened the effect by reading an elaborate statement of the New York State Librarian, showing that nearly every civilized Nation had, sometime or other, employed Negroes as soldiers and always with success, and winding up with the example of Brazil, the largest slaveholding empire of the world, using regiments of slaves at this very day as among the best soldiers they have. Alexander S. Diven [Rep., N.Y.] begged to trespass on Stevens' time, just to say that he had long been profoundly convinced that Congress failed in its imperative duty, just so long as it failed to provide for enlisting Negro troops to serve in unhealthy regions to which they had become acclimated, and he now had a bill to that end prepared and was ready to offer it at the first opportunity. That, resumed Mr. Stevens, is precisely what I would have done long ago, only I wasn't a conservative, and so they'd have called it an Abolition scheme. Stevens then went on with unusual earnestness and force, to urge the necessity for using Negroes to save white men. He declared that all over his State, households were everywhere desolated today because we hadn't troops enough, and now they wanted to call on them for more, to be sent into unwholesome climates, where exposure was certain death to any white man, and asserting that while such a policy was pursued, the suppression of the rebellion was hopeless. The effect of the discussion was seen when at the close of Steven's speech, the House laid Wickliffe's motion on the table by a vote of 74 to 29.

There will be no more sneering at Hunter's letter or his Negro brigade.

The President's Attitude*

1862, August 5

The President's refusal to accept Negro troops excites surprise among the parties interested in General Jim Lane's plans. Lane stated positively that the Administration understood his intentions about enlisting Negroes in Kansas when they gave him his powers for recruiting there. If that is correct he must have been treated in bad faith. Lane will probably go on and do what recruiting he can in Kansas and accept what Negroes he can get as camp laborers.

It had been hoped that certain features of the interview with the President yesterday on the subject of armed Negroes would not be made public, but garbled statements in a semi-Secession New York paper necessitate the publication of the facts. A delegation of Western men including two U. S. Senators made an offer of certain Negro regiments to the President, to which as stated last night the President replied, he had decided not to arm Negroes. The

* A telegraphic dispatch from Reid appearing in the *Gazette* of August 6, 1862.

matter was then dismissed with reference to Lane's project and the general policy. The President was plied with arguments against his decision, and the discussion gradually became warm. He finally exclaimed: "Gentlemen, you have my decision. I have made my mind up deliberately and mean to adhere to it. It embodies my best judgment, and if the people are dissatisfied, I will resign and let Mr. Hamlin try it."

To which one of the Senators replied, "I hope in God's name, Mr. President, you will." The heat of the discussion seems to have arisen from the feeling that the President was drawing back from the ground his visitors thought he had given them reason to believe he occupied.

The Liability of Negro Troops*

1862, August 21

Gentlemen here, who have recently returned from Cumberland Gap and other points where our Western armies are stationed, more than confirm your statements today concerning the probability of losing more than we gain by employing Negro troops. The names of several Kentucky Colonels are freely mentioned who have declared they would at once resign if Negro troops were sent into the

* This section is from Reid's New York *Times* correspondence, which he maintained for several months during 1862.

field, and their whole regiments are declared to be imbued with the same feeling. In some of them the declaration was common that they would at once lay down their arms should the Government arm Negroes as soldiers, while some have even gone so far as to say that in that event they would go over bodily to the other side. The East Tennessee troops are declared to be entirely free from such feelings or intentions as these, but it is insisted they fairly express the purpose of a large proportion of the Kentucky volunteers.

Six Days' House Debate

1863, February 2

Two months ago bills for enlisting slaves in the Southern States and mustering them into the National service had been before the House. Six days ago they came up in the regular order of business, the original bill by the leader of the House and John Hickman's [Rep., Pa.] amendments and additions.

The scenes that followed, the factious opposition that for eighteen hours of uninterrupted session kept the clerks calling yeas or nays on dilatory motions, the triumph of the determined majority, the keen debate that followed, and the final action on the memorable subject are worth a closer scrutiny than we ordinarily accord to the proceedings of our turbulent "popular branch." Let us take some time to look in upon this strange scene that—at the close

of the second year of the war for the supression of the
rebellion, and in the last month left the existing Congress
wherein to do whatever the times and its convictions of
duty demanded—at such a period for six long days was
enacted by the Representatives of the Nation.

It is Wednesday morning—damp and gloomy. The attendance in the House is but thin; in the galleries thinner;
in the reporters' gallery (best barometer for important
business you can find) thinnest of all. Nobody knows of
anything special that is going to happen.

The *Journal* is read—nobody listening; the Speaker sub-
mits a letter from the Interior Department of Indians—
nobody listening; the regular order of business is demanded—nobody listening; the Speaker announces the
regular order to be a bill to raise additional soldiers for the
service of the Government—very few listening, but they
listen very intently. William P. Sheffield [Rep., R.I.]
moves its reference to the Committee on Military Affairs
and on that demands the Previous Question. The Opposition suddenly prick up their ears. There must be some sort
of a cat under the Previous Question's mealtub! John A.
Bingham [Rep., Ohio] sharply demands a call of the
House. More and more suspicious! Clearly there's some
thing in the wind.

The Clerk bellows over the roll. Sixty or seventy members are absent. The doors are ordered closed, and the
names of the absentees are called for excuses. Half an hour
or three quarters is thus spent. The doors are reopened; the
crowd of tardy members outside pours in and flows down
the aisles; the business before the House is restated from
the Chair; the call for the Previous Question is not sec-
onded; and the Chairman of the Military Committee keen-

ly watching his opportunity cries, "Mr. Speaker," and gets the floor.

He appeals to the gentlemen having this measure in charge to let it be referred to him; says it clearly needs revision and that the Military Committee is the place to revise it; cleverly raps the Leader over the knuckles for wanting to engross all the business and time of the House, and closes by playfully hoping that he hasn't incurred his displeasure by these remarks as he would rather have that of ten devils at once.

The surly-looking old Leader responds—with a biting sarcasm, of course—whoever got the better of him at that game?—adds that this subject was referred (in substance) to the Military Committee two months ago and to this hour they haven't acted on it; and now he proposes to wait no longer. And the Previous Question is again called. . . .

Mr. Wickliffe crabbedly cries "Mr. Speaker." The Speaker rather tartly announces that debate is not in order. The modest old gentlemen, having so many claims to the kind consideration of the majority by reason of his own uniform courtesy, appeals for unanimous consent to talk. A desirable laugh almost downs the sharp cries of "I object" from the Administration side; and the old gentleman with a snappish air that would bring down the pit, if he were on the boards, resumes his seat.

Nothing remains but to permit its friends to take charge of the bill. In ten minutes the desired amendments can be inserted and the bill passed. Further delay cannot change the inevitable result and is but a childish waste of precious time.

The Speaker announces the main question. The piping tones of little Mr. Samuel Cox [Dem., Ohio] break out; "I ask to be excused from voting on this question." Well you may ask it, little demagogue, remembering the District you have! A Border State man of the Southern type—fit ally for the Columbus member—demands the yeas and nays on excusing the gentleman from Ohio, and the requisite number (of Peace Democrats, of course) second the demand. Mr. Vallandigham chimes in with, "I ask to be excused from voting on the question of excusing my colleague." The Chair rules the request out, and an Indiana sympathizer (William S. Holman, [Dem.]) instantly appeals from the decision of the Chair; while on Horace Maynard's motion to lay the appeal on the table, another Indiana recreant (James A. Cravens, [Dem]) demands the yeas and nays.

The game of the opposition is disclosed! The vote on the passage of the bill is already obstructed with a dilatory motion, and factious appeal from an acknowledged just decision, ruling out another, and on each the yeas and nays are demanded. An hour's wearisome calling of names is thus already interposed.

The purpose is manifest. Henceforth it is a contest of physical endurance. The minority have it in their power to delay the bill till the 4th of March if they have the physical strength; and already they are arrogantly announcing in the little groups all over the floor their intention to do it.

The Clerk rattles away over the yeas and nays; some Members answer to their names, more do not; confusion reigns throughout the Hall; as fast as one dilatory motion is disposed of, a couple more are piled up in its place; and so amid stentorian calls over the roll and merry motions to delay, the afternoon creeps slowly away. The Democracy are showing us how to do it. They are illustrating to the country their idea of the Constitution as it is and Congress as it should be. The Country will do well to note the illustration.

Sturdy John Hickman [Rep., Pa.] rises, with a face much longer than the moral law, to a question of privilege. "It is perfectly evident," he says, "that we have to sit all night with Kentucky"—"order, order, object, order, order," clamorously rings out from the Opposition side. "Please to find out what I am saying first," coolly retorts the collected and unimpressible Pennsylvanian. "I was about to move that, as it is perfectly evident that we have to sit up with Kentucky and the Border States all night— the gas be lit, that's all!"

The proper officers take the hint—in an instant the thousand gas jets above the ceiling are turned on, and a flood of soft radiance pours down through the stained glass, illuminating the Chamber as if it were high noon.

And so, without dinner or supper after six hours' continuous calling of Yeas and Nays, the tired House enters upon a night session.

You can pick out the new Members in an instant. Happy in their innocence, they are delighted with the prospect. Parliamentary cross-firing all night will be glorious, and they plunge into it with the zest of beginners. The elder heads don't seem to think it half so funny. They've been through such scenes before and have never found them specially enjoyable. With lazy smiles of content at the eagerness of their unsophisticated brethren, they retreat to the cloak rooms, stretch themselves out on the sofas, or recline on rows of chairs, and proceed to make themselves as comfortable as they can for the night's siege. If their votes are wanted, the young Hotspurs in the Chamber can come and wake them up!

The galleries which have been moderately full all afternoon begin to thin out rapidly. The Yeas and Nays are not interesting especially after dinner time. The Correspondents and Reporters go home for their dinners; a number of the older Members, who thoroughly know the ropes, slip out before the doors are closed to do the same. . . .

The Republicans, through the original ill-judged zeal of the friends of the bill, have thus been forced into a change of base, but the issue is still fairly made up. They mean to amend the bill and then pass it; the Peace Democrats mean to oppose the bill at every stage of every trick of factious opposition, and they choose to begin on the attempt to reconsider the Previous Question in order to amend.

There is no mistaking, then, the real nature of the contest. It is not the odious features of the bill they are fighting; it is the bill in any shape; and though they know its passage is a foregone conclusion, they are willing to devote days and nights out of the few precious hours that remain wherein to work in idle brawls, while the house is burning to delay the predestined permission to everybody that can, to throw on water!

Hour after hour creeps slowly away. One clerk relieves another in calling the yeas and nays. The members gather in easy groups among the desks, throw their heels up on top of their papers, discuss the gossip of the town, tell stories, crack jokes, and bandy repartee; while over all sound the sepulchral tones of the Clerk, intoning the roll-call.

But here comes an unexpected variation. A Democrat

demands the yeas and nays on some motion just made. "Shall the yeas and nays be ordered?" demands the Speaker in the accustomed formula, and enough ayes are clearly heard to order them. But the Republicans think they may as well take a hand. Colfax, always genial and ready for jokes, shouts, "Tellers, Mr. Speaker—Tellers." The Democrats look amazed. It takes a fifth of those present to order the yeas and nays, but Colfax must certainly know they have that many present. But the Speaker names the Tellers, and they take their place in the middle of the broad aisle in front of the Clerk's desk. The Democratic managers bustle about to whip everybody into the ranks. Crabbed old Mr. Wickliffe is punched up from a comfortable snooze and made to hurry down and pass between the Tellers. The tired old gentlemen stretched out on the sofas and in the cloak rooms are shaken up and pushed into ranks. The whippers-in rush down to the liquor shop in the basement and bring up the exhausted worthies who have been seeking to renew their faith at those perennial fountains of Democratic strength.

Their whole force is mustered (not all in the best of humor at the interruption) and marched between the Tellers. That done, they sing out, "Now bring on your men, and see if you can beat that." "No, no," says Colfax with a broad grin, "We give it up! We only wanted to give you a little exercise." The Republicans roar—the Opposition sulkily refuse to see the point.

After a tedious roll-call, a fresh motion comes up, and the yeas and nays are again demanded. "Tellers," again shouts Colfax, and Tellers are again appointed. With ill-concealed disgust, the Democrats repeat the process. Vallandigham, Henry May [Dem., Md.], William H. Wads-

worth [Constitutional Union, Ky.], George H. Pendleton
[Dem., Ohio] and Mr. Samuel Cox fly around hardly so
satisfied-looking as the last time, muster their whole
strength again, rolling everybody off the sofas, shaking
every body out of the chairs and getting the whole sleepy
flock through the Teller once more. "Now, let's see you go
through the funny process," growls Vallandigham. "No, it
isn't worth while," cooly returns Colfax; "we give it up!"

Another tedious call over the Roll, another fresh motion, another demand for yeas and nays and the Clerk is
just beginning the roll, when some Republican still again
sings out, "Tellers, Mr. Speaker." This is too much. "D--n
your Tellers," exclaims an enraged Democrat with hearty
emphasis; but the amused Republicans are inexorable, and
the Democrats once more have to abandon their lounging
and trot down the aisles between the Tellers—only to hear
the Republicans complacently "give it up" as they stumble
back to their seats, and the Clerk begins the roll-call.

Midnight approaches. Scarcely anybody had had anything to eat since breakfast. The Democrats have as little
faith in fasting as in prayer; and so, from the restaurant
below they order up a bountiful supply of crackers and
cheese to their cloak room.

One o'clock has arrived. Cyrus Aldrich [Rep., Minn.]
looks up at the clock, and, with the most innocent manner
in the world, inquires "Mr. Speaker, hasn't the morning
hour expired?" Which was pretty good—for Aldrich.

The monotony of the roll-call is absolutely distressing,
Roscoe Conkling breaks in upon it in disgust. He asks leave
to make a suggestion. "Agreed" shout the sleepy Democrats, and they flock over to the Republican side to listen.
"I suggest," Conkling begins. "I object," says Lovejoy.

"Oh, don't, Lovejoy, don't, don't!" appeal the Democrats; "Let's hear his suggestion." "If you're going to make this a fight, keep it a fight," responds Lovejoy; "I object to any suggestions." "Well then, let me ask a simple question," pleads Conkling. "I object," doggedly responds the Radical, with a half-surly shake of his good natured phiz, "let them take what they've bargained for!" Conkling sits, the disappointed Democrats return to their seats, and the roll-call drawls on.

Speaker Galusha Grow [Rep., Pa.], worn out with the exhausting demands of twelve hours' continuous session, has completely broken down. He calls Colfax to the Chair, and retires to the cloak room.

Presently Mr. Vallandigham, exhausted with the contest into which they had entered so gleefully, suggests a compromise and declares he has been opposed to this from the start! He moves to adjourn! Here is a ray of light. But up starts Mr. David Voorhees [Dem., Ind.]. They will not adjourn, he declares, if there are to be any conditions whatever binding their future action. Grandfather Wickliffe is now moved to deliver himself. He will eat, sleep, and drink here, in this Hall from now till the 4th of March before he will yield one inch to the majority in this matter.

The tired Clerk begins the roll again.

The galleries are desolate. Two disconsolate-looking women alone occupy them. Are they wives of members, who have come up to see why their truant husbands have deserted their bed and board?

It is five o'clock in the morning. Half an hour ago Wadsworth of Kentucky suggested that he would like to propose a compromise, at which innocent confession everybody got in a better humor. . . .

At last Thaddeus Stevens, the oldest man in the chamber and the freshest, comes in from the cloak room with a crowd of leading Republicans and Democrats following. He gets the floor without objection, and everybody listens. "Some gentlemen have been in consultation, and they think a vote on my motion to reconsider may be taken tonight to be followed by immediate adjournment." "Agreed, agreed," shout the Democrats.

It is precisely what the Republicans have been contending for ever since Stevens entered his motion to reconsider between seven and eight o'clock in the evening. The Democrats practically surrender; and even Mr. Wickliffe thinks better of his determination to stay there till the 4th of March and isn't heard to say a word.

... The "Night Session" is over. It is twenty-five minutes to six o'clock in the morning. It has been snowing and melting all night, the streets are covered with horrible slush; the streetcars stopped running five hours ago; and not a hack is to be seen; and most of the members are a full mile from their lodgings. May they have a pleasant walk of it.

The hour for meeting again approaches. Members, despite their last night's vigils, are early in their seats;—red eyed, sleepy-looking, but eager to see it out. . . .

Mr. Lovejoy's Rejoinder

Like an ancient and venerable bull when a red rag is thrust before his eyes, Mr. Wickliffe always commences pawing and bellowing whenever Mr. Lovejoy comes in his way. And, to do the latter gentleman full credit, he isn't very far behind. Each serves as the red rag to stir up the other. Lovejoy never says anything Wickliffe don't feel called upon to answer; Wickliffe never gets off one of his offensive, arrogant speeches without being goaded to madness as he sits down to see the broad grin with which Lovejoy invariably rises to poke fun (and pins) into him.

Today as always Mr. Lovejoy is true to the rule. He is on his legs and claiming the floor almost before Mr. Wickliffe's closing sentence has been uttered. Everybody laughs and turns to listen.

He begins, gradually, measuredly, in denouncing the factious opposition to this bill. Pretty soon Mr. Wickliffe gets a blow, and the very first one brings him to his feet, begging permission to interrupt! The gentleman from Kentucky has been consistent as well as persistent for from the first outbreak of this rebellion, every note and speech of his has proclaimed that he would rather see the Union perish than Slavery injured.

The first cut has brought blood. Mr. Wickliffe roars out something in response in accents so enraged as to show that the words reached the quick. Lovejoy instantly retorts, "Will the gentleman say so now, if one must necessarily be lost to save the other, which would he save, Slavery or the Union?" Wickliffe, instead of answering tries to parry the thrust by asking a question of his own, to which Lovejoy promptly hurls back an answer and renews his demand. Wicklife *makes no reply*.

Soon Lovejoy touches on Wickliffe's contemptuous way of speaking of Hunter and Butler, and his courteous allusion to that traitor Twiggs; and coolly adds, "Oh, Sir! a fellow feeling makes us wondrous kind!" The House and galleries (by this time crowded) roar, and Wickliffe, springing to his feet with unusual vigor, exclaims "The gentle-

man will allow me—" "*No sir,*" says Lovejoy with emphasis, "not unless you'll answer the question I asked you!"
"Well, go along! The country knows you, and it knows me
too!" "Yes, that's true, thank God for it," returns Lovejoy
in his blandest tones and with his most provoking
smile. . . .

The imperturbable "radical" continues: "Would I arm
Negroes? Ay, sir, not only would I arm Negroes, but I
would arm mules and make them shooting machines to kill
rebels if I could."

He is interrupted from another quarter; A portly Indianian in the back part of the hall . . . would like to make a
few remarks right here. The interruption is a little unusual
and unexpected. Mr. Dunn, though a Republican, has
always been thought remarkably conservative. Is he going
to make any trouble by opposing in any way the passage
of the bill? . . .

"I have been averse [said Dunn] to the employment of
Negroes. I thought there were loyal white men in the
South on whom we could rely. In that, thus far, we have
been disappointed; but we find abundance of loyal black
men. Why then not use *them?* The gentleman asks how we
can exchange them if taken prisoners and speaks as if
offering to exchange a black man for a white one would be
a great outrage on the white population. I tell the gentleman," and he hurls it out with a vigor Mr. Wickliffe
evidently thinks quite personal, "That a black man who
fights for my country, is *better than any white man who
fights against her!* One would suppose that, if the gentleman's own son was fighting in this war, he would rather
have him shot by a white traitor than saved by a black
loyal soldier! Sir, I *have* a son in this war and I am entirely

willing that black men shall help him subdue the white rebels. . . ."

"But the rebels shoot down Negro prisoners, and the gentleman asks, what will you do? *Make white traitors answer in blood for blood!* Every man who fights for our cause must be treated as a soldier, no matter what the color of his skin."

And so he takes point after point of the objections to the bill, and with a single stroke of his sledge-hammer logic, demolishes it. He has the unbroken attention of the House and the applause of the crowded galleries as he proceeds. This is no smart special pleading, no trick of demagogue oratory. Here is a finely balanced, unusually calm and judicial mind, wrought up to white heat. The allusions to his son and brother and nephews (for nearly all his nearest blood relations are in the army) have brought out the highest and noblest exercise of his ample powers; and the mental machines, without jar or friction but running at a speed that fairly exhibits its remarkable capacity, is with wonderful force and wonderful condensation, covering the whole subject with an armor of fact and logic that no attack can penetrate. The effect is superb.

He drives the last bolt home with a blow that resounds in applause through the chamber and galleries, and with courteous thanks to the gentleman from Illinois, resumes his seat. He has spoken but ten minutes, but he has covered the whole ground and made the best speech of the debate. . . .

A little clamor of "Mr. Speaker" from all parts of the Hall, a dozen gentlemen leaning forward and waving bills and papers at the Speaker to catch his eye; a few raps from the gavel; the Speaker announces the "gentleman from

Kentucky," and from all sides Members cluster around the honored figure of John J. Crittenden.

With a graceful bow and a courteous half deprecatory wave of the hand to the disappointed aspirants for the floor, the vetern in public affairs begins.

He speaks gracefully, of course, as is his wont; courteously toward those who differ with him as he always does; earnestly as a high spirited, aristocratic Southerner may be expected to do on such a subject. He has lost none of the old elegant fluency that all his life has passed for eloquence; none of the happy but stereotyped forms his forcible retort and repartee were wont to take in earlier years. And yet this is not the Crittenden we all remember—not the Crittenden our proud Harry of the West in the fullness of his days proudly introduced to the Senate as the man Kentucky chose to fill *his* place—not even the Crittenden that, in that magical burst of eloquence that recalled the memory of the Great Commoner he succeeded, denounced the iniquitous repeal of the old Compromise of 1820. The outer semblance of Crittenden is here, words still come in the old familiar phrases, responsive to the biddings of the intellect; but the voice can scarcely be heard over half the Hall—the fire is gone out—he is a weak old man.

Like other old men, he repeats himself. It is the same speech he has periodically made for the last year or two—but half changed to adapt it to the subject of debate. Of course he opposes the bill. He has all the proud, haughty feelings of the Kentuckian; he believes in *blood,* and as he says with a flash of the old spirit, he *stands up for his race against all others.* It would be unworthy of a great people to rely on slaves for their own defense. Sparta and Athens were warlike communities, but they kept their slaves, even white slaves, in their proper servile positions. Catiline, in all the depth of his depravity, even Catiline scorned to ask slaves to fight his battles. Shall we become baser than they?

That is the keynote. We need not follow him. The flame is weak and flickering—sometimes it flashes up with all the old brilliancy—but on the whole it is painful to listen to him and remember him in other days. . . .

He is a gallant old man from a gallant State. Glorious memories cluster around that almond crowned head; many of us have been proud to follow his leadership through former contests. He may lose our support now, but he cannot lose our respect—our love.

Judge Kelley Responds

Another clamor of "Mr. Speaker." and "the gentleman from Pennsylvania" [William D. Kelley, Rep.] is announced. . . .

[Judge Kelley touches] successively the arguments that have come from the other side of the chamber. Thus he disposes of one: "Why should it not be done? Is the life of the Negro more sacred than that of the white man? Why should not American Africans encounter the power of the enemy in the malaria of the swamps? Why should your son and my brother and our friends die that the Negro may live? I do not esteem him one whit better than ourselves, nor do I deny that he is our equal in right before the great God, our common Father, and in the great forum where absolute justice prevails. He is not better than we and should share the dangers and sufferings of this war." . . .

As we listen to the eloquent sentences and watch the more eloquent manner a strange illusion comes over us. This is not the babling Congress of small men, thrust upon these great times of ours; this is not the chamber where unused stump-speeches are habitually discharged at unoffending listeners; and this man is not made of such material as we use for Congressmen.

The ornate walls take different form and more gorgeous hues; the galleries become the dress-circle of beauty and fashion in our proud Queen City; the desks fade away; the members become the occupants of the pit; the roof expands and rises and flashes down radiance from sculptured form and painted beauty; the orator is before the footlights in our princely Opera House; we are listening to the superb rendering of some grand old Roman Senator's words by Edwin Forrest*—or better, by our own matchless James Edward Murdoch*.

Or, rather, the actor carries us even *beyond* the glowing illusions to which we are used. This is not Murdoch showing how Cicero denounced Catiline it is Cicero himself; and these are Roman senators listening spell-bound to their first of orators. . . .

These are high praises, but they are deserved.

Another Day for it.

Friday morning reveals the presence and earnestness of the House. The members were up all Wednesday night, and sat through an exhausting session the next day again; yet

* Popular actors on the American stage.

the debate once more opens with a full House as well as with crowded galleries.

The kind reader has been very kind if he has followed me thus far; I cannot ask him to listen to today's talking at length. And especially may we afford to skim it over as the fire of the debate has gone. There are good speeches still—able, forcible, well-put. The galleries are still interested and occasionally respond with vociferous applause. . . .

Saturday's debate is still less interesting. . . . Mr. Carey A. Trimble [Rep.] of Ohio, surprises even his friends, with a speech of unusual power and eloquence. Mr. Trimble talks so little that members had hardly given him full credit for saying so well what he did say. It is a capital speech and makes one regret all the more the sad slaughtering he received at the hands of his friends last fall in being thrown into a hopelessly Democratic District. Still, he may redeem that in time as he did his old one. Mr. Trimble is of a Virginia family, nearly all his relatives are in the South, and most of them doubtless in the rebellion; and to crown all, he married in the South, too. It requires some strength of conviction to make such a man advocate of this bill; yet he does it and does so forcibly as to receive the warmest congratulations of the members generally.

Another day's protracted debate, the House this evening passed Thaddeus Stevens' Negro regiment bill by a vote of 83 to 55. Before its passage, Samuel Casey's [Rep., Ky.] amendment was adopted, providing that the slaves of loyal masters in the States excepted by the President's Proclamation should not be enlisted, and that no recruiting offices should be opened in such States except on procuring consent of the Governors thereof. The bill itself gives permission to enlist any number of Negroes not exceeding three hundred thousand, to be paid ten dollars a month with rations and equipments to be officered by white men. On the passage of the bill Jacob B. Blair and Joseph E. Segar [Unionists] of Virginia dodged; Benjamin F. Thomas [Conservative Unionist] of Massachusetts, William Kellogg of Illinois, Hamson* of Ohio and Valentine B. Horton [Rep., Ohio] voted against it.**

1863, February 6

Senator Henry Wilson [Mass.] has passed large numbers of applications from officers desiring commission in Negro regiments and brigades. He thinks that a Negro army 100,000 strong could easily be officered by white men in less than a month's notice, just as that first news of the New Year's proclamation of freedom was brought to New Orleans by colored Unionists from Port Hudson.

1863, February 14

The abstract of the [Senate] bill contemplating the organization of the Negro army, which was telegraphed you some days ago, differs as printed in one or two particulars from the bill as introduced by Mr. Sumner. The

* Possibly Richard A. Harrison, a Union Democrat from London, Ohio. No Hamson represented Ohio at this time.
** This last paragraph comes from Reid's telegraphic dispatch and not from an Agate letter.

pay of these soldiers is to be $7 instead of $11 as the sum was changed on the wires and the bounty of twenty-five acres of land to the officers and ten to the privates is to be located upon lands confiscated during the rebellion, not reserved by the Government for public use and to be occupied only as a homestead by the person entitled to receive the same.*

How Not to Get Negro Soldiers

1863, April 2

We have all been rejoicing over the brilliant reports that come to us from the Negro brigade in Florida. It is no longer a question whether Negro troops are valuable, and Negro enlistments already receive a new impetus.

And yet the historian of these times will write it down as a remarkable illustration of the *meanness* which marked our policy, that to this day every Negro we enlist goes into the field with a halter around his neck, and we have not the manhood to take the simplest measure for removing it.

The rebel threat to turn over to the soldiers for execution or to the State authorities, to be dealt with under State laws, every Negro taken in arms remains untouched

*This and the previous paragraph are also from Reid's telegraphic dispatches.

and emphasized by the brutal massacres of Murfreesboro'. Every Negro who enlists does so with the prospect
of being sold into Slavery, if captured, staring him in the
face as the mildest fate he can expect.

What redress do we aver? We talked very bravely when
the Negro enlistment bill was up in Congress. "Every
enlisted man must be treated as a soldier, no matter what
his color; and if he is not so treated, then blood must
atone for blood." But the rebel order remains unrepealed;
its barbarous execution in every instance where they have
had the opportunity to execute it, remains unavenged; and
still, offering them tenfold the dangers our white soldiers
incur and none of the protections, we ask Negroes to enlist
in this war and fight for their liberties!

They naturally hesitate at becoming soldiers without
being secured the treatment of soldiers. What then? Do we
guarantee to them what is so clearly their right? This great
country, so tender of its soldiers, so jealous of their privileges and rights, instead of encouraging these Negroes it
seeks to enlist by pledging them the ordinary securities of
war—without taking any steps to prevent them from being
murdered or to protect them in rebel prisons, proceeds in
certain districts to *draft every able bodied man of them!*

Yet we *have* touched one lower depth of meanness on
the same subject! It is when the poor Negroes in the North
having no bounties to stimulate their patriotism save these
prospects of being murdered or sold into Slavery, hesitate
about volunteering to encounter infinitely greater perils
for far less reward, and we vent our disappointment by
exclaiming, "We told you so; of course they won't fight;
they're only poor, cowardly Niggers anyway!"

How Philadelphia Raises Negro Soldiers

1863 June 22

We are in one of the Loyal League club houses, and the Executive Committee of the Union party is in session, discussing the means for setting in motion the plan for raising a brigade of Negro soldiers. There are some questions of pay and bounty and the like which seem still involved in a little uncertainty, and it is decided to refer them to the War Department for solution. It seems settled that the Governor is to have nothing to do with commissioning the officers and that the negro troops are to be in no way subject to State control; but there is not the slightest aversion to having the State credited with their numbers in filling up her quota. It is conceded that, to raise these troops as rapidly as is desired, considerable extra expenditure will be necessary; and the Philadelphians are talking of raising ten to twenty thousand dollars as an additional fund for hastening the enlistments in each regiment.

It is worth while to notice that these men thus earnestly devoting time and money to "turning niggers into soldiers" are not Abolitionists—at least as we used to call Abolitionists three years ago. They are not even Free Soldiers—scarcely, indeed, Republicans. The solid men of Philadelphia, representatives of her wealth and conservatism, and knowing no party title but Union men are here, and they are going into this work for the defense of the State, for calling out a valuable element of their military strength, for relieving by so much the burdens of their white popula-

tion—in short, these practical men are undertaking it solely
as a practical business matter. What a change! Scarcely six
months ago, to advocate the arming of a Negro was to
horrify all the respectable conservatives of the Union party
and to furnish the opposition a weapon so formidable
against us that from all quarters there came up to Congress
last winter earnest appeals to Union members not to commit themselves to so suicidal a folly. The day for raising a
panic over Negro enlistment has passed; and it, like confiscation, emancipation and a dozen other bitterly denounced "Abolition measures," has passed as an accepted
fact into the history of the war. It is no longer a theory or
an experiment, and it has ceased to be a party question—in
Philadelphia at least.

The Right to the Land

1864, April 7

The Secretary of War is responsible for a new legal idea.
Such things are not so common as to be passed over
without notice; and so far as I know, this is absolutely
new.

The slaves, he argues, have the strict, technical, legal
right to the land of the rebels.

He undertakes to establish it thus:

They have always had one right, which constituted a
legal lien upon the property, personal or real, of their
masters—the right to subsistence. The masters may be

gone, but the property remains—still subject to this lien held by the slaves. Under the principles of the Confiscation Law, the right of the master to his estate is gone. No other parties have any claim to it; no others have any interest in it, *save the slaves who still have their lien.* In legal language this is the remainder in interest.

It is a well established legal principle that, where there is no other title, any sort of a lien gives possession and title. Therefore the slaves holding the only lien have the legal right to the property.

I do not know that the Secretary, who has been amusing himself by setting forth this theory in conversation occasionally, regards it as a very good law according to the books, but if it isn't, it ought to be!

Public Transportation

1864, January 19

Washington has been full of strange illustrations of late, of the burial of prejudices under the avalanche of change the war has wrought; but I know of no stranger one in its humble way than a curious little fact connected with a street railroad. When it was begun two years ago it was poison for a white man to breathe the same air with a Negro in a street car or omnibus. Let the storm be as pitiless and the car as empty as you chose, the Negro woman with a bag in her arm must stand on the front platform and bear it, lest her presence in a corner within should contaminate the scattered passengers. By and by it began to be suspected that perhaps the Negroes might be entitled to ride within if they had cars to themselves; and the suspicion became a very strong one when it was found it would pay.

That was a few months ago. This morning I rode down to the Capitol in a car labelled, "Colored Persons can ride in this car." It was crowded with ladies and gentlemen who a year ago would have been horrified at such a position; and by their sides sat the Negroes to whom the car rightfully belonged! The whites had actually taken possession of the Negro car, and the most aristocratic ladies sat beside well dressed Negroes without a shudder.

In its casual way I know no happier illustration of the discovery that many have been making, that worth has as much as color to do with what is respectable and what is not.

Citizenship*

1864, December 23

The submission to the President's wish for the recognition of the reorganized State of Louisiana by the Congressional Committees on the rebellious States removes

---

* An Agate Dispatch not in the Reid Collection appearing in the *Gazette*, December 28, 1864.

nearly all the difficulties that have seemed likely to hinder an early adjustment of the question of Reconstruction.

One other point, however, is still the subject of careful debate in the committees. Who shall vote in the reconstructed State Governments? Not the disloyal, certainly— that would but be removing the war against the Union from the battlefield to the safer arena of Congress. Yet how can you have a sufficient voting population without these disloyal men in many regions where it is safe to say that every white man over the age of eighteen has been an active rebel? Shall the only loyal class, the Negroes, be admitted to vote? And if so, will you give the most ignorant fieldhand in Georgia and South Carolina knowing absolutely nothing of the Government save that "Massah Linkum hab set us free" the same power in shaping its destinies with Edward Everett or Thomas Ewing?

On the whole it is well that the question comes up in this precise shape, and now Congressional Committees (and indeed Congressmen in or out of committees) are not noted for their courage; but difficult as it is to meet the question thus presented, they will now be apt to find it more difficult not to meet it. We may well congratulate ourselves therefore if the necessities of the hour shall force Congressmen to a discussion (be the discision what it may) of the common sense and really republican feature that ought long ago to have been embodied in all our State Constitutions: "Every male over 21 years of age who shall be a native of the country, or who shall have been a resident five years, and been naturalized, and who shall be able to read and write, shall be entitled to suffrage, and no others shall be."

Then and Now—Arming the Slaves

1865, February 22

Less than two years ago, the vinegary-faced ex-Governor of Kentucky, [Charles A. Wickliffe] who then preserved in all its purity the model of plantation manners in our House of Representatives, was vigorously declaring that the insanity of our propositions for arming Negroes could only be equaled by their utter absurdity. "Make niggers fight!" exclaimed the testy old crabbed-face, "You might as well try it on monkeys! I tell you one white man, their master, (pronounced as if written "moster",) would make a whole regiment of them run away!" To join him in such vehement protests the old man vinegary found such allies as John J. Crittenden, almost the whole border State delegation, and the bulk of Northern Democratic Congressmen.

That was as I have said, less than two years ago, and there are little slippered pages flitting to and fro today on the floor of the House, who can remember the debate.

The Richmond papers received today announce the determination, in secret session, to arm two hundred thousand slaves, and we know that already the conscription of slaves for this black army is rapidly going forward! Are those who stood in the nation's way, and sought to the last to do the dirty work for slavery in our legislation—are those poor fools answered?

Six months ago this rebel determination might have cost us dear. But they are the most foolish who are wise *too late*. If the good fortune that any management but the blindest must now insure does not desert us, the rebel remedy for these present ills will be ready only after the patient is dead. Let Sherman once join Grant, unshattered, and Lee might as well be organizing a joint stock company for a railroad to the moon as a black army.

VIII

Reconstruction

Reid's comments on reconstruction parallel the fortunes of Chase's effort in the winter of 1863-64 to gain the Presidency from Lincoln. By March, 1864, when it was clear that Chase could not draw significant support, Reid ceased to comment on reconstruction. Chase's ideas for the new southern governments were obvious in many dispatches.

The Second Confiscation Act

1862, July 9

"Sir," said Mr. Sumner, in closing his recent eloquent plea for Confiscation in the Senate, "the present Congress has already done much beyond any other Congress in our history to entitle it to the gratitude of the Nation. . . ."

The Senator was right. The present Congress has doubtless its weaknesses and its faults; but its record thus far is brighter and more hopeful than has been that of any of its predecessors since the earlier and purer days of the Republic; and it is not unnatural that, as their work approaches completion, the members should point with just and honest pride to such a summary of what they have accomplished.

The appropriation bills are passed; most of the absolutely essential measures of legislation are disposed of; and of all the important questions that demanded the consideration of Congress, but five [four] remain— . . . a new Tariff, Confiscation of rebels' slaves, provision for bankrupts, and a policy for the Government of the Seceded States as they shall be reconquered. . . .

For governing the Seceded States as they are reconquered, there is now one bill before the Senate—that by Judge Ira Harris of New York, "to establish Provisional Governments in certain cases." Some measure of the sort is felt to be a necessity. Thus far the Government has been groping along without a policy and with inconsistent practice. In Virginia, a third or less of the population of the State have been allowed to reorganize the government and carry it on for themselves. In Tennessee a Brigadier General has been detailed from the volunteer service to govern the conquered territory under the military law. In North Carolina we have a military Governor who holds no military position, and as the Senate strenuously insists, no position of any kind, and a similar arrangement has been made for the little strip of South Carolina we occupy.

It is thus manifest that we are progressing utterly without a policy and equally manifest that some uniform mode of procedure must be adopted, or reorganized State Legislatures and Brigadier Generals commanding States and Military Governors without commission or duties will all come to grief together.

The Military Governor business received a sufficiently ridiculous illustration in the recent Stanly-Colyer difficulty which showed that "Governor" Stanly was utterly without instructions or duties except to act as a sort of missionary to the North Carolin heathens, and to try and encourage them to come back—certainly the vaguest task ever set before the "Military Governor" sent out to direct the affairs of a great revolted State. But recent discussions in the Senate have brought out this fact that even those general powers are unwarranted. It seems that Mr. Stanly has no commission as "Governor" or as any other sort of officer; that there has been no law authorizing such an office, and that his appointment has never been sent to the Senate for confirmation.*

The whole subject of governing and restoring the Seceded States is thus at loose ends, and the necessity for some law becomes more pressing than ever. Judge Harris' bill may possibly be yet crowded through at the present session.

The Winter of Hope

1863, September 29

A month's absence gives no new charms to the Capital on one's return. . . .

Several things combine to make people look forward to next winter as one of the most important periods of our history. It is the winter before the Presidential nomination and campaign; and its plans and developments will mea-

---

* Lincoln appointed Edward Stanly, a former North Carolina Congressman, as Military Governor on May 19, 1862. Overly conservative, he received little support from either Lincoln or Congress and resigned in May, 1863.

surably decide to whose hands shall be committed the adjustment of the troubles that are upon us. It is the winter that all seem to unite in regarding as the turning point in the war, that is largely to shape its future course and results. It is the winter in which a new Congress organizes; in which the old financial problems come up with new and more difficult conditions; in which above all the whole question of the RECONSTRUCTION OF THE UNION and the policy on which it shall be attempted seems likely to be presented and moulded if not decided.

Reconstruction-But What Type?

1863, November 25

For many reasons the approaching Congress is looked upon as likely to prove the most important in our history. It is now almost certain that the President will bring before it at its coming session the question of reconstruction. In any event the question is bound to come up, and this Congress must settle it. . . .

Save straggling guerrila bands, Mississippi and Louisiana are clear of rebels in arms—are reconquered. What are we going to do with them, govern them as conquered provinces or restore them to their places as States?? Something we must do, they cannot be left without government. What shall it be?

In Arkansas and Tennessee the question is equally pressing. We hope it will soon be in Texas if not also in North Carolina. What shall we do with these States? Mr. Stanton

is understood to have declared that they will consent to
the appointment of no more military governors; shall we
have provisional governments organized by Congress, or
shall these people quietly reorganize again under the old
regime, as some of them modestly proposed the other day
to do in Louisiana and return their Representatives and
Senators to resume the balance of power in Congress?

These questions do not relate to something in the far-
distant future, they are already upon us. Some sort of
answer will be called for, and given, in the approaching
Congress.

It is possible that the war may not be so near its close as
many imagine, but that does not remove the instant pressure of these problems. If our arms do not progress one
foot in the next twelve months, we still have to provide for
the territory already regained. If we treat it as conquered
territory, as Mr. Sumner proposes, that is deciding upon
our course. If we hold that the loyal people constitute the
State, and, prescribing the tests of loyalty, allow them to
reorganize their governments, as Mr. Chase proposes, that
is deciding upon another course. If we allow the former
citizens indiscriminately to reorganize, as Mr. Blair, the
tories, rebels and the rest propose, that is deciding upon
another policy. But *some* decision, it is apparent, cannot
be long withheld. The discussions that precede it are likely
not merely to form the burden of Congressional work and
to shape the issues of the approaching Presidential election, but to become to this nation in all its future history
what the debates on the formation of the Constitution
have been to its past.

Of the other multiform questions of general policy, of
the proper management of the army, of the direction to be
given our naval development, of the financial measures to

be adopted for the limitation and final extinction of our
National debt; one need not speak. They will combine to
give to this Congress a responsibility from which the wisest
may well shrink. Add to all this that we are on the eve of
the conventions that are to nominate the next candidates
for the Presidency, and that the doings of this Congress
will have much to do in shaping the course of the contest,
as well as the fates of its leaders, and we surely have
elements enough for an exciting winter.

Secretary Chase on Reconstruction

In the whirl of the election enthusiasm in Ohio last
month, I do not think the fact was generally noted that
Mr. Chase, in his Mozart Hall speech, had really defined his
views on some of the points involved in the question of
Reconstruction. As these views are likely to form the text
of much discussion, and may form a crystalizing point for
the parties on these new issues, I copy, from the revised
report, the paragraphs containing their pith:

> ... All that is needed is to recognize the plain
> indisputable principle, that in the regards of the Na-
> tional Government, *the loyal citizens of a State con-
> stitute the State.* ... Is there a man here who wants
> these noble, faithful, generous men to go back to be
> trampled under foot by restored rebels? [Cries of No,
> no!]

The Mozart Hall speech, from which the above is an
extract together with Mr. Chase's other speeches on his
western trip, have been collected, thrown together with a
running narrative of the trip, and published by the Grand
Council of the National Loyal League, in a handsome
36-page pamphlet, just out.

The Thirty-Eighth Congress

1863, December 8

Thirty eight Congresses have assembled during our national existence. Of these, three will stand out in History with peculiar prominence. One is the Congress that first met at the birth and sought to shape the growth of the infant nation. Another is the Congress that found the same nation, now grown to stand among the first in the world, attacked by a rebellion formidable beyond precedent; and was compelled on the instant to improvise means for its preservation, by inaugurating the greatest civil war of modern times. And the third is the Congress, just assembled, whose high privilege and responsibility it will be to bring back the rebellious portions of the nation, after these fierce convulsions, to settled and orderly Government.

The organization of this last Congress will be an event in History; perhaps we may find it interesting to watch it as it progresses.

Lincoln's Message on Reconstruction*

1863, December 10

This document [the President's message] will command the attention and respect of the country and of

---

* Not an "Agate" Dispatch, but a "Washington Report" by Reid. The President's message, according to T. Harry Williams, both

the world. The great question of the crisis—the settle-
ment of the rebellion, the status of the black population, the redemption of the State Governments from
treason, and their regeneration under loyal authority—
he meets in clear and straightforward manner. . . .

The President speaks with no uncertain sound. He
lays down a policy in plain language, not elegant in
style, but beautiful for honesty and truth; and there
is in it the inspiration of a religious trust in the
prevailing power of principle, and of perfect confidence in the support of the American people.
                                    —*Gazette* editorial, December 10.

The first reception of the President's Message was quite
favorable. As they began to scan it more closely, the
radical wing of the Administration party became more
cautious in their praise.

It is regarded as decidedly settling Montgomery Blair's
claim to have spoken for the President in his Rockville
speech. Nevertheless Blair is said to express satisfaction
with it.

It does not endorse Sumner's views on reconstruction,
yet the friends of the latter claim that it substantially
includes and embodies them.

The pivotal point of the whole message is the idea that
absolute, complete emancipation will at length be the basis
of reconstruction. The proclamation is in itself supposed
to be of little avail without important congressional legislation. If Congress takes up the question at all, therefore, the
subject of reconstruction must form a large element in this
winter's debates, notwithstanding the efforts which have

"please and puzzled" the Radicals. *Lincoln and the Radicals*, (Madi-
son, Wisc. pb. 1965), 301.

been made to stave it off. It is now seen, while Secretary Chase's Mozart Hall Speech did not exactly indicate Mr. Lincoln's views, it came nearer to foreshadowing his policy than any other utterance either from a member of the Cabinet or others. Mr. Lincoln's friends claim that the Message will prove one of the most popular State papers ever penned. The Democrats, on the other hand call it a cunning trap, smacking rather of the attorney than the statesman, and deny that it originated with him besides. The intense radicals express something of the same opinion, in saying that it owes its apparent popularity to the avoidance of the points on which he knew anything he would say would arouse differences among his supporters.

Louisiana

1864, January 23

The work of "reconstruction" is at last practically begun; and as is not unnatural, it does not begin without some dissension. General Banks' order of the 11th inst., by this time published everywhere, shows under what auspices, and in what way it is proposed to reestablish a loyal State government in Louisiana. A letter, telegraphed from here the other day, showed in language probably neither temperate nor quite just, the views of the Free State men who differ from General Banks.

The points at issue may be briefly stated:

1. The gentlemen controlling the great Free State mass meeting, held in New Orleans on the evening of the 20th

inst. looked upon that as the last of a series of measures preliminary to a movement for modifying the Constitution and reorganizing the State Government *by the spontaneous action of the registered loyal voters.* General Banks has chosen rather to inaugurate this movement *under military authority.*

2. Some of the leading Free State men deemed it of especial importance that delegates to a convention to amend the Constitution should be chosen before a State election was held. General Banks has reversed the order, and fixed the State election for the 22nd of February, while that for the Constitutional Convention is postponed to the 1st Monday of April. This, they say, leaves the measures for wiping out slavery undetermined, while the State Governments organize under the old pro-slavery Constitution.

3. Some of the Free State men object to an election of members of Congress till after the Constitutional Convention shall have redistricted the State.

Jealousies of this sort seem to me the easiest explanation of the complaints forwarded here from New Orleans. Nothing has been said about them in the papers; but, besides the letter sent by telegraph, I have seen others of the same tone and tenor, addressed to high Government officials. Some regret is manifest at the difference of views in Louisiana thus indicated; but all hands will undoubtedly sustain General Banks; while every effort will be made to hush the complaints and bring the dissatisfied free State men into hearty cooperation with him.

I do not see that any theory of reconstruction has been adopted here beyond the outlines given in the President's Proclamation. Within the limits of that Proclamation, General Banks seems to have been allowed to adopt in the main such measures as seemed to him best. Very probably similar discretion will be given to other commanders. But, in some way or other, it seems to be understood that before summer two more States, at least, will be reorganized, and represented in Congress.

Congress has as yet done nothing to fix any policy on the subject; and meantime events seem to be shaping a policy for themselves. With the arrival of Congressional delegations from these States, the subject will be opened in the broadest shape. Presidential considerations will begin, too, to mingle with it, for the electoral vote of these States may go far toward deciding the election. With such interests involved, it is natural that the opening steps should be closely scrutinized.

Arkansas

1864, January 25

The policy of reorganizing the State Governments in the rebel States under the old pro-Slavery constitutions, seems to have been definitely adopted by the President.

When General Banks disappointed the Free State leaders of Louisiana by insisting that they should postpone their convention to amend the Constitution and make it squarely anti-slavery, till after they had organized their State Government under the old Constitution, it was supposed by some that he was acting on his own responsibility in this particular; or that it was only an isolated case. But General Garnett and the rest of the Arkansas delegation came on here, making the same request and have been disappointed by the same reply.

I do not know that any particular principle is involved in the point; but these loyal people all express the fear that, in organizing under the old Constitution and laws, the half-and-half Union men will get the uppermost, and we will have a return to the old "conservative" system that, after the Revolution, was to wipe out Slavery tenderly, and did it by expanding it southward and westward, wherever it could go.

But I began simply to note the fact that thus another step in the process of reconstruction seems to have been decided upon by the Executive. And so, whether for the best or not, as the hand of war is stayed, the work of rebuilding the shattered Governments begins. May its results be as happy as its beginning is propitious!

The Bayard Test Oath

1864, January 26

Of course the whole significance of the recent protracted debate in the Senate on what has been popularly called the Bayard test-oath, lay in its bearing upon the question of "Reconstruction."

If men who enter Congress must swear that they have

never given aid or comfort to the rebellion, then all such are forever excluded. On the other hand, if men who *have* given aid and comfort to the rebellion are admitted, what security have we that we shall not meet on the floor the rebels we have conquered on the field—that, abandoning the effort to maintain their cause by arms they may not without let or hindrance renew their old struggles for it in the House and Senate? In one word, without the oath, what security have we that John C. Breckenridge should not profess to have seen a great light, and come back to the Senate, from which he was expelled—that James Mason and R. M. T. Hunter should not renew their old blustering dictations, that men fresh from the fields, where they have cost us the lives of our best and bravest, should not abandon arms for courts, and quietly resume the old struggles when tired of the new ones.

It would be hard to say that a couple of our western Senators, of approved fidelity and devotion, or that one from Pennsylvania and one from New York who, although "conservative," have never been supposed to be worse, meant to bring about such a result; but is it not the legitimate tendency of their votes?

The matter here is constantly connected with the "reconstruction" movement initiated in Louisiana and the one in preparation in Arkansas. It is useless to conceal that many of our best men are skeptical as to the existence of a sufficient number of thoroughly loyal men in at least one of those States to warrant an effort at reestablishing its Government now; and that from more than one quarter there comes the inquiry, why all this haste in giving up the power we now have over these States?—why this anxiety to restore to them, before we know how or where they stand, the power to do as they please again?

Waste and Haste

1864, January 30

A good deal of unnecessary time was wasted yesterday in the House on the question of the right of the bogus members from Louisiana to admission.

But one of these members had the assurance to remain to prosecute his claim at all. The others, after an ineffectual attempt to befool the Sergeant-at-Arms into paying them mileage and salary, found their means exhausted and beat an inglorious retreat to cheaper regions and more gullible people. The one who remained claimed to represent a district that, at the last apportionment, contained ninety-three thousand souls. He was barely able to prove that *one hundred and fifty-six* votes had been cast for him! And on the strength of this "election" he had the hardihood to demand admission into the House of Representatives! Could the broadest farce go further?

And yet this pretender, whose name Mr. Emerson Etheridge (after rejecting Winter Davis and half a score of others duly elected) placed upon the roll of the House, was suffered yesterday to speak till he was exhausted in defense of his claims, and on Tuesday he is to try it again. If the House has much respect for itself, it will make short work with him.

Some opposition begins to be manifested in Congress to the theory of reconstruction, on which the Administration is beginning to work in the rebel States. Louisiana has an election for members of Congress called for the 22nd of February. Arkansas is soon to have one. And it is intimated that Tennessee and Mississippi, if not also Texas, are not likely to be long behind.

And yet, in the debate in the House on this very question of admitting the Louisiana claimants, Mr. Nathaniel B. Smithers [Republican, Delaware] took occasion to say that he objected to their admission solely because there was no civil government in the State, and a Military Governor held possession of it. It is difficult to see how the Congressmen to be elected under General Banks' proclamation could escape the same objection. Mr. Thaddeus Stevens took even stronger ground, declaring that the members from New Orleans admitted at the first session had no shadow of legal right to their seats. And several others have made remarks that it is well to continue to hold these rebel States under military government for the time,—"for half a century, if need be," one said,—until it is certain that, when a government *is* organized, it will be in the hands of loyal men. . . .

If I add to this that the apparent haste to bring in several of these States again, and to commit their government to a tenth part of their voting population, is a topic of comment, and in some cases of animadversion in Administration as well as Opposition circles, I think I have fairly stated the way in which the subject is regarded.

It must be said, however, that many of the sincerest friends of freedom in and out of Congress rejoice in these efforts to reorganize certain State Governments within a

month or two, and regard them as the most auspicious
signs of the triumph we are achieving.

Garfield on Confiscation

1864, February 19

There was a striking little picture in one of the closing
passages of General James A. Garfield's late speech on
confiscation, to which many a soldier's eye will again and
again revert:

"I want to see, in all these insurgent States, the men
who have fought and suffered for the truth, tilling those
fields on which they pitched their tents. I want to see
them, like old Kaspar of Blenheim, on the summer even-
ings, with their children upon their knees, pointing out the
spot where brave men fell and marble commemorates it."

It has been a common remark that emigration always
follows the lines of latitude; and simply because it *is*
common, and, in the main, uncontradicted, most men have
come to believe it. But it is not true. The whole history of
Europe, from the time that northern barbarians overturned
the old empire that Constantine supposed was to be endur-
ing, and planted their families upon its ruins, down to the
invasions that made our Anglo-Saxon lineage what it is,
presents one continuous evidence of its falsity. Or, if you
seek for illustrations on other continents, to this day the
Chinese Empire is crossed by a wall that runs *east and
west.* It was built to resist an invasion from the northward,

and built in vain, for Tartar emigration followed the triumphant Tartar arms.

Periods of convulsion and of general war show again and
again the same results. The hereditary craving of the Czars
for the possession of the Porte is but an expression of the
universal desire of northern men for warmer climates. Or,
as Kinglake* has happily expressed it, "Men dwelling
amidst the snows are driven by very nature to grow covet-
ous, when they hear of the happier lands where all the year
round there are roses and long sunny days."

I do not mean that like conditions exist *here,* with those
that from the earliest ages have in the Old World led
emigration southward or southwestward; but these cases
are enough to show that there is no natural law carrying
emigration along the lines of latitude; and that with us, for
three quarters of a century it has been the accident of our
situation rather than a fixed law that has so directed it.
There were broad prairies and rich mineral treasures to the
westward, free to all. Southward the lands may have been
as rich, but the hardy emigrant had no inducement to
explore it, while at the threshold he was met by a system
with which he would not bring his free labor to compete.
And so Louisiana, Mississippi, Arkansas, were given over to
the broken down planters from the seaboard, who sought
to repair their wasted fortunes by finding cheaper lands.

But with the peace that cannot now be very distant
there comes a change; and it is in precisely this connection

---

* Alexander William Kinglake wrote an eight-volume *History of the
Crimean War*. The first two volumes were published in 1863.

that the confiscation question becomes practical or inter-esting at all.

Men say that, as it now stands, the confiscation bill amounts to little or nothing. It is probably very true. They say absolute confiscation is impossible, for the President will veto it. It is possible though not, I think, probable now, nor of much moment anyway. What the President undoubtedly would have done at the last session it is by no means so certain that he would do now. The circumstances have changed, and in all our history no man in place has so promptly responded to circumstances. But in any event, no man can stand in the way of events. Confiscation of the landed estates of rebels is as certain as the end of the war is certain.

And with the confiscation comes the marked change which statesmen and political economists and dealers in lands and young men seeking their fortunes must observe. For the next quarter of a century *emigration in this country goes Southward and Westward.* The tide of our civilization has reached the Rocky Mountains; it will next sweep toward the Gulf. The South is to be our "New Country" now.

IX

Politics and "Situations"

In December, 1863 Reid attended an organizational meeting preparatory to the Chase boom which was to give the Republican nomination in 1864 to Salmon P. Chase. The plan miscarried and Lincoln easily got the nomination. Such activity on Reid's part was not to be detected from the "Agate" Dispatches, which continued to be clear and incisive comments on the political and military scenes. Toleration of Lincoln, praise for the radicals, and confidence in Union arms were dominant themes of the Dispatches after Gettysburg and Vicksburg. All Dispatches were written from Washington unless otherwise noted.

Anna E. Dickinson

1863, June 22
from Philadelphia

Yesterday evening Judge William D. Kelley,* the eminent Philadelphia Congressman and orator, was good

---

*Kelley, mentioned in Chapter VII, was later better known as "Pig Iron" Kelley for his advocacy of a high protective tariff on iron and steel.

enough to call and propose playing the chaperon to us a few hours today. . . .

[The day] was so pleasantly passed that I cannot resist the temptation to live it over again by writing about it. . . . We are presented to Miss Anna E. Dickinson, the young Quaker girl to whose wonderful oratory the gallant Republicans insist that our triumph in Connecticut is due. . . .

To begin with, this is no scrawny-featured, sallow-faced, pantalooned female of forty of the woman's rights persuasion, but a *girl*—a few months over twenty, the old Quaker women, headed by Lucretia Mott and the other Quaker authorities on age, say—scarcely eighteen, *our* equally practised eyes decide on the instant. Plump, round, supple figure of about medium height with graceful outlines half-concealed by the neatly fitting dress, glossy black hair, cut tolerably short and falling in luxurious profusion about the neck and curling away from a low, broad forehead; deep eyes, of a dark hue you can hardly define, contracting and dilating in the excitement of the animated talk; a broad, rich mouth, with ripe lips that curve into a score of expressions in an instant; a square, (not masculine but still) firmly set chin that gives a hint of the persistent purpose that has brought this girl up through all manner of difficulties to a position almost as proud in its way as that of Mrs. Stowe—certainly far prouder than Mrs. Stowe had attained at twenty, or thirty either—there is an inventory of the features, set down as drily as you would write out the multiplication table.

I need hardly add that, without being strictly classical in its outline, the face is beautiful, and the expression of course charming. Add to this the wonderful personal magnetism she is said to possess on the platform, and the brilliant character of the speeches themselves as they are reported in the papers, and you have ample explanation of the enthusiasm she aroused even in hypercritical New York. . . .

"Noctes Ambrosianae"

In the evening I was fortunate enough to meet Miss Dickinson again at tea at the elegant residence of a friend in one of the suburbs of the city. Her career . . . seemed to me so wonderful that even the *blase* interest of a professional journalist was aroused to see what *could* be the elements of this remarkable popularity; and if I studied her rather in the light of a rare specimen of natural history than as a well-bred and accomplished young lady, that woman's failing, curiosity must be my excuse. . . .

Of course she is radical as all women of culture are likely to be (from Margaret Fuller to Mrs. Stowe to Mrs. Browning), and of course, like all other women, she sometimes jumps to illogical conclusions without any bother of reasoning on the road. It was amusing to see how demurely she received a remonstrance against some of her complaints about the slow progress and hesitating steps of the Administration along paths that seemed to her so plain, and how she swallowed her dissatisfaction like a dose of medicine, and promised to try to see things on their most hopeful side. Not less amusing was it to see her flame out into an invective (not quite just) that on the platform would have carried any audience off their feet against the accidental refusal of a Negro company in the height of the week's panic at Harrisburg; and, to a toughening old bachelor, inexpressibly ludicrous to see the intense (and very sincere) rage with which she denounced some luckless speaker who had insulted the whole female sex by calling ex-President Buchanan an old woman in pantaloons!

But enough! This young girl, so brilliant, so magnetic, so wonderfully gifted, is a real genius; and God gives us so few of these, we may be pardoned the rudeness of talking about them in the newspaper.*

The Public Debt**

1863, July 29

During the periods of National gloom through which we have been called to pass in the progress of the rebellion, nothing has so alarmed our sincerest patriots or furnished the Tory Democrats such effective arguments against the

* Reid's affair with Anna barely survived the Civil War. After that they maintained a friendly relationship until 1876 when Anna began a career on the stage. Reid's able but overly conservative drama reviewer, William Winter, attacked her so viciously in the New York *Tribune* on her performance as an actress that she believed her career in drama was ruined because of it. To the end of her life she believed that Reid was partly responsible for the severity of Winter's attack and her subsequent failure on the stage. See Girard Chester, *Embattled Maiden*, (New York, 1951), pp. 182-90, 267-68.

** This dispatch indicates that Reid's later harping on the debt question as managing editor and editor of the New York *Tribune* was motivated by political rather than economic reasons.

war as the rapidly increasing proportions of our National Debt.

. . . Many accepted the loose statements of declaimers and prophets of evil, and straightway concluded that we were saddling ourselves and posterity with an enormous debt, which could never be paid; that the mere interest would keep up a perpetual drain upon our treasury; that our expenditures amounted to fabulous millions per day and were constantly increasing; that repudiation was much more likely, indeed, than any effort to pay even the interest on the debt; and that in short we were hurrying along the high road to National bankruptcy.

Even within a month I have heard earnest and intelligent Union men, holding prominent official positions, declaring that another year's war would swell the public debt to such frightful dimension that we would be forced, either to pay the soldiers by settling them on the lands they had conquered, or to repudiate the whole of the war debt under a Democratic administration, to be brought into power on that distinct issue.

An instant's reflection would have shown the last apprehension to be utterly groundless. Our debt is in great measure a popular loan, scattered broadcast by fifties and hundreds and five hundreds among the well-to-do farmers and mechanics and shopkeepers in every State and almost every county of the North. The Seven and three-tenths Loan was taken almost exclusively in this way, not by the capitalists, but by the masses; and at this very time the Five-twenty Loan, after a success utterly unprecedented for months, is still passing out in small sums, fifties and hundreds, at the rate of over a million a day. Are the people likely to repudiate debts thus owed to themselves?

In this very characteristic, indeed, of our financial policy lies our chief security. Referring to the forebodings of the alarmist in England at the portentous growth of the British debt, during the great Continental war, Macaulay said:

> They erroneously imagined that there was an exact analogy between the case of an individual who is in debt to another individual, and the case of society which is in debt to a *part of itself.* They were under an error not less serious, touching the resources of the country. They made no allowance for the effect produced by the incessant progress of every experimental science, and by the incessant efforts of every man to get on in life. They saw that the debt grew; and they forgot that other things grew as well as the debt.

There are many marked differences between the nature and growth of the British debt and our own; but Macaulay's observation applies quite as well to our case as to their own.

But can we ever pay our present debt, much less the probable debt a year hence?

On this and kindred points a little *brochure* by Dr. William Elder of the Treasury Department, recently published by the Philadelphia Loyal League, furnishes so complete and satisfactory answers that I cannot do better than give copious extracts from it—which was indeed the purpose for which I began this letter.

Dr. Elder's statements are fortified by official authorities in all cases; and full tabular statements give the arithmetical operations by which his conclusions are reached. Omitting these which have stood the severest scrutiny, and are still open, in his pamphlet, to the critical examination of any who may be disposed to assail them, I give merely the results. [Reid then quoted extensively from Elder to show that the debt could be paid without too much difficulty.]

Vallandigham*

1863, October 14

Thank God! the good name of our noble State is once more free from stain! It was a disgrace to Ohio, loyal mother of us all, that such a man as Clement L. Vallandigham could be nominated by any considerable party of her citizens for any respectable position in the State; but right nobly has the disgrace been wiped out. Our People forgot Party when Patriotism was involved; and from the River to the Lakes their condemnation of Traitors and Sympathizers with Traitors has sounded out in tones so clear, so loud, that through the whole limits of this Nation, rebel or loyal, none can fail to hear.

If Ohio furnished the most conspicuous and persistent minion of the Great Rebellion, Ohio, too, has magnifi-

* This is an editorial by Reid appearing in the *Gazette* of October 14, 1863. Reid had reported Vallandigham's speech to the House of Representatives in January, 1863 and the "Vallandigham Convention" in Columbus, Ohio in June, 1863. Reid frequently commented on this famous copperhead's activities.

cently repudiated her recreant, banished Son! No, exiled *citizen,* NOT Son! Thank God! he is no Son of Ohio, whom her People have loathingly spurned from his crouching position beyond her border.

Beneath our office windows the people of Cincinnati are thronging the public space in a wild exuberance of ecstatic joy they have not shown since the first proud victories of the war stirred the great heart of the Nation to its profoundest depths: and the name of the candidate whose high honor it has been to become the symbol of a State's loyalty is ringing in exultant shouts from square to square.

"Count every ballot a bullet fairly aimed at the heart of the Rebellion," said the great Minister of Finance yesterday. They are counting the bullets thus truly aimed! In the morning the State will count from our bulletins as the City counts tonight; and as the reckoning is footed up, there will come a gush of joy and of pride that overtops the joy.

It is no great victory that prompts this thanksgiving of the Commonwealth. It is simply the redemption of our fair fame! It is what we all knew the noble State must do, but what it thrills us to find she has done so superbly.

The estimates we thought the wildest are far outstripped. The State Central Committee talked of thirty-two thousand majority on the home vote. It will be fifty thousand! At Columbus they say it is more likely to be seventy-five thousand! And this is without our Soldiers! Wait till their voice comes in, and the thunders of our home guns will be penny firecrackers beside the reverberating roar of their artillery. . . .

So much for the Victory! And now the retributive justice it compels!

It has been no ordinary contest concerning disputed

questions of politics. It was a grave attempt by certain leading men, enjoying the privileges of citizens of Ohio, to establish Treason to the Government under the forms of law—to place the State in direct hostility to the Central Government. For that crime and for all the consequences that crime would have entailed, had it been as successful as they strove to make it, we hold these men responsible now and through all their lives. For *this* sin there is no forgiveness.

Political opponents from whom we differ we can yet esteem; but men who sought to degrade the Nation by base submission to its enemies or to dishonor the State by placing it with the traitors against the Government—why should they be less infamous evermore than the Tories and Cowboys of our earlier and less dangerous times of trial?

The prime mover in all this conspiracy is CLEMENT L. VALLANDIGHAM. Let *him* pass! Convicted by two courts, banished by the Chief Magistrate of the nation, an appellant from that tribunal to the bar of his State, and by her cast off with an ignominy none other of her citizens ever received—branded Traitor by the Rulers, sealed Traitor by the People—let him wander, outcast that he is, with the mark of Cain upon his brow, through lands where distance and obscurity may diminish, till the grave shall swallow his infamy.

Ohio has had Sons whom she delighted to honor; men crowned with her Senatorial bays, or chosen to stand and speak for her among the Representatives of the Nation. How had this foul rottenness festered in the state, that it could reach these men and blight them forever? In a moment of crazy delirium they permitted vexation at private grievances, or groveling fealty to party machinery

by which they hoped to rise, or unmanly fear of party drill
to conquer their consciences and their honor; and to the
horror of all who took honest pride in their fair names,
they fell to be the seconds and adherents of the malevolent
outcast. It is a hard fate for men who have had large
futures before them; but stern justice demands that henceforth, to each one who loves the honor of his State, their
names—they rise to all lips, we need not call them over—be
held INFAMOUS forevermore.

There can be, there must be no escape. They will seek to
evade the responsibility for their bold, bad attempt; will
shuffle and equivocate and deny; but it must not be. As
they have sowed, so must they reap. For the deceived
masses there may be many excuses; for the deceiving
leaders none. To have been a Tory in the Revolution will
seem a light thing in the years that come beside having
been a VALLANDIGHAM leader in the Great Rebellion.

The Recent Virginia Campaign

1863, October 21

"Forward and Back." The Dancing Master still gives
commands to the Army of the Potomac. Today it runs for
cover under the defenses of Washington; tomorrow it is
pressing hotly upon the defenders of Richmond.

The country cannot keep up with it; cannot arrange its
transports in harmony with the situation. The western
papers that reach us, three days old, are as amusing as Joe

Miller. They talk about a battle on the Rapidan when Lee is cozily established at Mannassas. Catching up with the events, they speculate on the danger of Washington—when Lee is running for dear life to Richmond and destroying the railroad behind him to delay our pursuit.

In truth the late movements here have been a farce. There is every reason to suppose that Lee valorously advanced on Meade—with a single corps! the latter took to his heels and started for Washington—the single corps lustily pursuing. General Warren unconsionably insisted on testing the mettle of this imposing foe, when presto! the trick was discovered, and *they* took to their heels!

Such seems to be the clearest statement one can give just now of the last "campaign" here. Its results are—some cost of horse-flesh and shoe leather and patience; the destruction of the Orange & Alexandria Railroad; and an enforced delay, under cover of which Lee may help Bragg, establish himself in the defenses of Richmond, evacuate the capital, or do whatever else may seem to him good.

There is talk now of Meade's removal; and complaint is especially based on his failure to follow up Warren's handsome blow. What a day may bring forth nobody can tell; when the most prominent Cabinet officers didn't know of Rosecrans' removal till days after it was ordered, one may be excused from pretending to predict anything; but it is certain that the President and the War Department have not been well satisfied with Meade's recent movements.

And this brings up Rosecrans. The telegraph has told how his removal has been received here, what stories have been started to his prejudice, what carnival of slander has broken loose over his downfall. One who has never believed him to be either Bonaparte or Julius Caesar, may the better now refuse to rush to the other extreme in branding him Patterson or Porter.

It is known that General Rosecrans' relations with General Halleck have not been the kindest and that the latter officer has sometimes regarded his subordinate as impertinently obstinate in his opinions and demands. And it is known that since Chickamauga there has been a flood of complaints against him (mostly from interested parties) pouring in at the War Office. Add to this that the President has for some time been contemplating some change in the Department, and we have the sum of public *knowledge* on the subject. The swarms of rumors of course are infinite.

Rosecrans' Removal*

1863, November 3

The removal of General Rosecrans from the command of the Army of the Cumberland has produced so profound

---

* This inside story of Rosecrans' removal was based on official correspondence Reid had somehow seen, possibly through the agency of his fellow statesman, James A. Garfield. Andrews, *The North Reports the Civil War*, pp. 471-72. Reid also sent the story to Greeley who, with better communications with the nation's capital and with faster typesetters, published it in the *Tribune* November 7. It appeared in the *Gazette* November 10 under the November 3 dateline.

Almost half a century later Reid wrote General Gates Thruston, a sensation while its causes have been so imperfectly or falsely stated, that it may, even yet be of some interest to put them on record in an authentic shape.

It is not wonderful that the general, who took the disorganized and discouraged Army of the Cumberland in mid-Kentucky, swept on with it from Bowling Green to Nashville, to Murfreesboro, to Tullahoma, to the Tennessee, to Chattanooga, without one step backward, without losing one foot he had won, should have such a hold on the hearts of a grateful people that his removal should produce a painful shock.

It need scarcely be said that the stories of General Rosecrans' drunkenness, his opium-eating, his liability to epileptic fits, or his religious depression are alike utterly, wholly, maliciously false. The War Department has never entertained any such charge or harbored any such impression. It is due to General Rosecrans that this should be said in the fullest and most emphatic manner. For, whatever may have been his errors, this man has done the Nation

---

". . . all that I have ever written about it [Chickamauga] was from second-hand information, largely from General Garfield, General 'Jim' Steedman and other participants. I had served as a volunteer aide on Rosecrans's staff, in his early West Virginia campaign; and probably a sense of personal loyalty to him led me in editing this second-hand information to give more credit to the stories of Rosecrans and his friends than of the other side." To Archibald Gracie, author of *The Truth About Chickamauga*, he added that "Garfield was actuated by the same impulse and did his best to defend his chief—an effort which met with little reward from Rosecrans himself in later years." Reid to Gates P. Thruston, to Archibald Gracie, December 19, 1911, Reid Papers, Library of Congress.

such signal and distinguished service that all loyal men will be tenderly jealous of his fair fame.

The irritation and dissatisfaction in the War Department and at the headquarters of the army, which have resulted in General Rosecrans' removal, have been of slow growth and their origin is to be sought for many months back. Chickamauga was merely the occasion, by no means the sole or chief cause of the removal.

There were two main sources of this irritation—one the military management after Stone River down to Chickamauga; the other the unfortunate complications and suspicions created by the army police system, which General Rosecrans persisted in sustaining against all remonstrances. Of the first:

I. The War Department was first surprised, then anxious, and at last openly indignant, at the delay after the victory at Stone River, which, in spite of every representation of the urgent necessity of action, stretched on for month after month from New Year's until the last of June. In general terms, it complains that, with his army in good condition, he wasted at least five months, doing nothing, while on either side of him our armies were sorely pressed, and his advance, by relieving them, would have won victories, not only in his own Department, but East and West as well. Complaint, developing into indignation, is particularly expressed at his failure, notwithstanding the earnest appeals of the President, the War Department, the General-in-Chief, and General Grant, to move on Bragg at a time when that officer was known to be materially weakening his army by sending reinforcements against Grant at Vicksburg.

Out of this failure grew an irritating correspondence

with the authorities here which very much increased that
dissatisfaction. Without quoting fully the language of any
one set of dispatches, scenes passed, of the tone and
temper of which this is a faithful reproduction: Secretary
Stanton would telegraph, "I am very much dissatisfied
with your long delay, and think, unless you move at once
the country cannot justify your course." General Halleck
would write, "I feel very kindly to you General, and have
the highest respect for the abilities you have so signally
displayed; but be assured that neither your reputation nor
mine can withstand the effects of this delay at a crisis
when the exigencies of the service so imperatively demand
movement." The President would write: "I am very much
grieved by your unaccountable delay. I am bound to
believe that you on the ground are the best judge of what
you can do but you see how vitally important movement
is, and you give me no reasons that seem to me satisfactory
for the delay." To all this General Rosecrans would answer, "I know what the country needs; and I know too
what the army needs. I must have my communications and
supplies secure. It has never been my habit to move into a
place until I could stay there. If I am not competent to
command the army you can remove me, but while I
remain in command I must use my own discretion and
move when I get ready." Such passages as this did not
occur once or twice only but systematically.

Sometimes it would happen that the War Department,
irritated by the general's conduct, and not fully understanding the obstacles with which he was contending,
would blame him severely for matters in which it was clear
to every one who understood the case, that he was not
blameworthy. No one who knows his sensitive and impul-

sive disposition need be told how this injustice always lashed him into a fury, and how indiscreet and haughty were his replies.

Thus the delay at Stone River and the irrating correspondence that grew out of it developed the initial cause of the War Department's dissatisfaction.

It is to be regretted that General Rosecrans did not cause the Department to thoroughly understand what reasons (whether sufficient or not) it is now known he did have for the delay.

At the time the pressure for a forward movement to relieve Grant began to be heaviest, he addressed a circular letter to all his corps and cavalry generals—fifteen in number—asking their opinion on three points: First, whether there had been any material weakening of Bragg's force; second, whether, if there had been, it was sufficient for us to fight a successful battle; and third, whether he, the general addressed, was in favor of an early or immediate advance. On the first point, the opinions were about equally divided; on the second, most inclined to the belief that we could not fight a successful battle; and every general answered the third by opposing an advance. One of them— a corps commander at that—went so far, after an advance had been finally decided upon, as to say that it would be the fearful and bloody mistake of Rosecrans' life-time. It was no light thing to attempt a movement with every prominent General he had thus protesting against it.

Finally, however, on the 12th of June nearly five and one-half months after his great victory, General Rosecrans decided to move. But he still delayed as it seemed to the War Department unreasonably; and it was not till the 22nd that the army was put in motion. The Department now has the indisputable evidence establishing beyond possibility of doubt, that for weeks if not months before this movement was made, Bragg's army had been so weakened by sending troops to Vicksburg, that he had but *forty-one thousand* men of all arms remaining; while exclusive of officers, Rosecrans had *sixty-five thousand.* This evidence, it claims, was either in General Rosecrans' possession or accessible to him before he asked the opinion of his generals.

But when he finally moved against the wish of all his leading generals, he handled the army so superbly and made so successful a campaign, that it was supposed the good reasons of the Department had for finding fault with his not moving would be forgotten in the brilliancy of his operations when he did move. Unfortunately, however, he had delayed till the June freshets were upon him. Bragg, retreating by turnpikes and railroad, escaped, while Rosecrans was toiling over the dirt roads by which he had to make his flank movement. Bragg was driven from nine miles of fortifications at Shelbysville and from five at Tullahoma; and all Middle Tennessee was relieved without a battle, but the War Department would not forget that but for the delays of which it complained the movement would have escaped the June rains and Bragg would have been crushed instead of driven. Thus the foundation was laid for future disagreements and grave dissatisfaction; while an enemy had also been made of the hero of Vicksburg.

II. Passing from the delay at Murfreesboro the Department found another ground of complaint in the delay at Tullahoma. It insisted that instead of halting there, he should have pushed right on to Chattanooga; and it re-

garded his procrastination from the first of July to the
middle of August as indefensible, injurious and criminal. If
the Department had remembered that the retreating enemy had burned the bridges, destroyed the railroad and
fortified himself in Chattanooga; that Middle Tennessee
was cleared *without* advancing beyond Tullahoma, and
that there could be no motive for going further except in
attempting to go right into Chattanooga; and that *this* with
a river half a mile wide, eighty miles of broken railroad,
the entire range of the Cumberland Mountains to cross,
and freshets that would have made even good roads impassable, was simply an impossibility; it would not perhaps
have blamed *this* delay as severely. But it had good reason
for complaint before, and without very closely scrutinizing
the altered situation, it was further aggravated and enraged
at what it regarded as a repetition of the same fault.

Most unfortunately for himself, General Rosecrans now
went to Nashville to inspect the garrisons and examine the
condition of his communications and stayed at a hotel
there two weeks. The Department instantly construed this
as arguing an utter indifference to its desires and the
pressing wants of the service.

All this time the correspondence had been growing more
and more sharp; and, as Rosecrans felt the injustice of
expecting impossibilities from him, and saw how utterly
the Department failed to understand the topography of
the country, his replies became vinegary and imprudent in
the extreme. Assistant Secretary of War Dana and General
Meigs both said to him that they thought they had studied
the descriptions of the country thoroughly, but, on entering it, found that they had no conception of its nature.
Rosecrans considered the higher authorities in their turn
more ignorant still, and treated them accordingly.

When he went to Nashville, the Department here determined that it must change its tone. Hitherto it had confined itself to suggestions and entreaties; now it became peremptory. Orders began to be sent instead of expostulations.

Under this spur, General Rosecrans returned, moved the army up to the Tennessee River, and completed his means for crossing it. This was accomplished between 17th August and 1st September. Considering the immense amount of work to be done, it is probable that greater speed could not have been expected; and the Department could not complain; but the old irritation continued, and the correspondence, continually growing more curt, constantly aggravated it.

III. This brings me up to the Government's third cause of dissatisfaction with General Rosecrans' military management—the Chickamauga campaign.

In the last days of August the Deparmment telegraphed General Rosecrans, peremptorily ordering him to cross the Tennessee at once, to report each day's movement of each corps, and to allow no twenty-four hours to pass without sending on a report. No orders were given as to where he should cross or what plan of operation he should adopt after crossing.

Two courses were open to him. He had a few brigades lying on the north bank of the river opposite Chattanooga. He could move the whole army there—cross the river under fire and storm the enemy's works, as Burnside attempted to do at Fredericksburg. Or, he could cross the river twenty miles below, and through some exceedingly difficult passes in Lookout Mountain, turn the enemy's flank— a movement that bore some resemblance to Hooker's attempt at Chancellorsville. In other words, he had either to fight the enemy out of Chattanooga by an attack in front, or to maneuver him out by a flank movement, *and then fight his way in.* He chose the latter.

It is precisely on this point that the public has utterly failed to understand the true nature and object of the battle of Chickamauga. The popular impression is that General Rosecrans by a skillful flank movement took Chattanooga and might there have rested, but that he got ambitious of further laurels, was intoxicated by his easy success, became as rash as he had before been cautious, rushed impetuously ahead, was caught off his guard, soundly pummeled, and sent back with a very bloody nose that his own indiscretion had secured him.

The truth is that General Rosecrans never really held Chattanooga until *after* that battle; that he had to fight at Chickamauga to get his army into Chattanooga.

Let me explain as briefly as I can.

The army was thrown across the river some thirty miles below Chattanooga. Between it and the rebel position stretched Lookout Mountain, a perpendicular wall of limestone, which no wheel could cross. The mountain juts up against the river, two miles below Chattanooga, leaving a narrow pass by the river bank, through which the railroad runs. To have attempted to march up to Chattanooga through this pass would have been madness. It were easier to cross the river directly in front, and storm the works. Nevertheless, it was the quickest way to get into the place—if the rebels would only get out beforehand.

Twenty or thirty miles out from the river (south) was the first gap in Lookout Mountain; twenty miles further was the second. The reader who fixed the location of these gaps has General Rosecrans' plan in a moment. He placed Crittenden's Corps near the river at the foot of the mountain, ready to march right up through the railroad pass, and so into Chattanooga the moment the rebels should leave it. Thomas' Corps he sent out along the mountain to the first gap, and McCook's to the second, with instruction to cross over as soon as possible. The moment the heads of their columns began to debouch on the other (Chattanooga) side of the mountain the enemy saw his danger. If he remained in Chattanooga, we were on his line of supplies and south of him. He evacuated at once, hastening southeastward to Lafayette [Georgia]. Crittenden, quietly lying a few miles down the river, of course, marched up through the railroad pass at the river's edge—no longer dangerous, with the enemy gone—and occupied the deserted stronghold.

But did this give Rosecrans Chattanooga? He held it very much as a straggler who should get away around to the enemy's rear could be said to *hold* the enemy's line of communications. He had but a corps there, which the enemy could crush at any time. Henceforth his whole effort was directed to getting his *other* two corps into Chattanooga so that he could reunite his army before a fight and hold his position. *It was in trying to do this that Chickamauga was fought.*

Crittenden was not strong enough to hold Chattanooga, so he was moved southward—*not,* as the public supposed, in pursuit of Bragg, but to get nearer the rest of the army, for safety against Bragg. McCook was ordered to close up on Thomas, then the two, still fronting the enemy at Lafayette, were to close up, moving by the left flank, on Crittenden; then the whole army, continuing the left flank movement, was to try to slip sideways into Chattanooga. For the enemy was known to be heavily reinforced.

Immediately after crossing the river, General Rosecrans

had telegraphed here: "I have repeatedly told you that the enemy can reinforce himself at will, and that he will be a great fool if he does not do it." It was now certain that he was *not* "a great fool."

McCook was twenty miles beyond Thomas. Thirty hours, or at most two days, were allowed him to reach Thomas' position. Had he performed the march in the time expected, Chicamauga would not have been fought, and the army would have got safely into Chattanooga. The order reached him on the 13th; by the evening of the 15th he should have joined Thomas, while it was not till the 16th that Bragg issued his general order from Lafayette, announcing to the army that it was heavily reinforced and ordering an advance "to seek the enemy."

But instead of moving directly down the plain mountain road, McCook, under some unaccountable delusion that it was not practicable, absolutely went back over the road by which he had crossed Lookout Mountain, and went down the valley to the gap through which Thomas had crossed; and so by this roundabout route came in on Thomas' rear, consuming five days instead of thirty hours in effecting the junction. Those five days settled the fate of the army. He did not reach Thomas till the evening of the 17th; on the morning of the 16th Bragg had issued his orders to advance; and the reinforced enemy, pressing forward and closing in, had already compelled Rosecrans to bring Crittenden still further away from Chattanooga, and clear up to Thomas' left, to save both corps from annihilation in detail.

As soon as McCook got up, General Rosecrans started the army for Chattanooga; but it was too late. The enemy struck the head of his column near Rossville [Georgia] on the 19th, and Chickamauga followed. Technically it was a defeat; but General Rosecrans still accomplished his purpose—he got his army into Chattanooga, though at a fearfully heavier expense than had been anticipated. If he lost the battle, he still won the campaign. And campaigns are bigger than battles.

I have been thus particular in tracing the operations preceding and producing Chickamauga, both because it is proper to correct false impressions as to the reasons why the battle was fought and because those false impressions had their effect in increasing the War Department's dissatisfaction with General Rosecrans' management. Until recently the real facts have not been understood here; and the Department, sharing in the public impression that the battle was the imprudent act of an overprudent man, grown suddenly ambitious of greater triumphs and rendered foolhardy by his easy successes, went as much further than the public in its condemnation, if [as?] its disposition to condemn had been more aroused by previous causes.

IV. But the dissatisfaction on this score was light compared with what I now name as the fourth and more immediate reason for the removal: General Rosecrans' voluntary separation from his Chief of Staff at the crisis of the battle, and his retiring, "stampeded," as Department officers are wont to express it, to Chattanooga, while the Staff Officer insisted on pressing forward to the front. The Secretary of War is understood to have gone so far in speaking of this, as to denounce it as an act of absolute cowardice. None of us, who remember the brilliant personal bravery with which the hero of Stone River has so illumined so many triumphant battlefields of this war, can fail to regret that any one should have so far forgotten himself and forgotten the bloody records of our glory as to harbor such an unworthy thought for an instant; but it cannot be wondered that General Rosecrans' unfortunate and inexplicable course should have finished the work the previous irritation had begun.

It will be remembered that a movement made by Brigadier General Wood under misconception of orders opened a gap in the line of battle, through which the rebels at once poured and pulverized the right of General Rosecrans' army. The general strove for three quarters of an hour to rally them, but in vain. It was while making this struggle that General Lytle was killed within ten or twelve yards of him. Meantime the advancing rebels had cut him off from his center and left, and he was carried back on the tide of the route to the foot of the mountain and made a detour of seven or eight miles. While doing this he met stragglers who said they were from James Negley's command, and that it was routed and retreating. He knew that he had sent Negley's troops to the extreme left. Accepting their story as true and leaping at once to the conclusion that if both right and left were routed, it was a hopeless defeat, he instantly resolved to hasten at once to Chattanooga and prepare to reorganize the straggling fragments.

It was the fatal mistake of his life. I do not know that his friends make any defenses for him on this point, except to say that it was an error of military judgment as to facts that, if his understanding of the facts had been correct, it would have been the very best thing for him to do; and that, at any rate, it is harsh to remove a distinguished officer for being on a single occasion deceived by false information from his soldiers.

The authorities reply that nobody but a man already "stampeded," as they phrase it, could have committed the mistake; that he might have known that he had left a portion of Negley's force, with Negley himself *on the Right* and that it was from this quarter the stragglers he questioned came; that at any rate the roar of artillery and musketry toward the Center, at the very time he decided all was lost, ought to have been proof conclusive that his army was still gallantly holding its ground, and should have spurred him *to* instead of away from it, and that this *was* conclusive to his Chief of Staff, as it should have been to any SOLDIER.

I do not pretend to enter into the discussion. It is enough to say that his unfortunate step convinced the War Department of General Rosecrans' incapacity for a sustained protracted effort to meet an overmastering crisis, and at once decided that he must not be left to command the greater number of troops now required at Chattanooga. Henceforth his removal was only a question of convenient occasion.

V. But there came still another cause. General Rosecrans drew his army within the lines of Chattangooa and evacuated Lookout Mountain (which General Hooker has recently retaken) thus giving up his line of communications on the south side of the Tennessee, and compelling the army to rely on opening a new road through the mountains to the northward. The Department regards it as unnecessary, and calls it a further result of his having been "stampeded." General Rosecrans regarded this point as too far from his main body to be defensible.

VI. This completes the several points of his military management which combined to produce General Rosecrans' removal. I have only to add, that the oldest and longest continued cause of complaint the War Department had against him grew out of his relations to a certain Mr. Truesdail, whom he had made chief of his Army Police. This person had been originally employed as a sort of mail agent at General Pope's headquarters at New Madrid and before Corinth. He is said to have been finally expelled by General Grant from that army—at any rate he left it under a cloud. Gaining General Rosecrans' confidence, he secured the right to sell newspapers in the army; and subsequently he rose to be appointed to organize a system of army police.

Whatever may have been his real merits or demerits, it is certain that nearly every respectable officer in the army, particularly among General Rosecrans' warmest friends, declared him an unsafe man for so important a place; and many of them did not hesitate to denounce him as a villain. The people and the State Government pronounced him corrupt and mercenary. He was charged with cotton speculations of an illicit character and with all manner of rascalities.

But he was remarkably shrewd; no evidence was brought against him sufficiently clear to convict him in General Rosecrans' eyes; and the latter, by no means insensible to flattery, was so played upon as to be led to believe implicitly in the honesty and skill of his Chief of Police. The complaints he regarded as persecutions; and so, the dogged obstinacy of his nature was aroused, and in spite of the remonstrances of his best friends, he stuck to Truesdail in defiance of every charge and suspicion. There was no evidence of any corrupt connection between them, and those who knew General Rosecrans will utterly scout at and repudiate the idea; but it cannot be denied that retaining him most seriously injured the general in the estimation of the Government and even compromised him with his own friends.

This was a distinct source of dissatisfaction here, combined with the accumulation of all the rest, aided in bringing the Government to the point of removal.

Add to all this that the delay at Murfreesboro had produced such a feeling between Rosecrans and Grant that they could not serve amicably together, and it is seen why, after it had been decided to place Grant at the head of the great concentration of our armies at Chattanooga, it was not possible to leave General Rosecrans in even the subordinate position which the commander of the Army of the Cumberland was thenceforward to have.

Such, then, are the causes of the removal which so startled the nation. If they are more grave than those of us who are friends to the justly distinguished general could have wished, they are at least not such as affect his personal honor, or detract from the well-earned reputation his previous brilliant services have given him.

A Little Official Light on Chickamauga

1863, November 6

There are one or two points concerning the battle of Chickamauga, which have never been understood here till the official reports cleared them up. One ... point is

General McCook's assigned reason for going to Chattanooga while the battle was still in progress. He says in his report that the last order he received from General Rosecrans was to support General Thomas, and having made his dispositions to that end, to report to him (Rosecrans) in person. General Rosecrans having gone to Chattanooga, he intimates that he followed him there to report. It is true that, after receiving this order, he had seen and conversed with Rosecrans in person on the field, but not having improved this opportunity to make his report, it is still technically true that when he came to do it he had to go back to Chattanooga in order to give a literal obedience to his order.

How the line came to break in the mysteriously sudden way it did on the right is also explained. It will be remembered that, passing toward the right, John Brannan's Division came next to Reynolds' and Wood's next to his— Wood's being not in line but in echelon. An aide appeared, apparently not understanding the echelon formation, and seeing what he supposed to be a gap between Wood and Reynolds, so reported to Rosecrans. The General, accepting the report as correct, at once sent an order to close up the line. The order appears to have been loosely expressed by the staff officer who wrote it out, and General Wood (Thomas J. Wood of Kentucky, Colonel in regular army) construed it as an order to withdraw from his place (where he was already beginning to be sharply engaged), pass to the rear of Brannan, and come up to the support of Reynolds. Of course that opened a gap through which the army might pour. The rebels instantly leaped into it, turned upon the weaker part of the line and were already scattering the Right like chaff before Wood had reached his new position. General Wood himself must have understood the effect of the order as he construed it, for he afterward said, showing it, "I hold in my hand the fatal order of the day." Some of General Rosecrans' friends, I believe, claim that he put a construction on it which even its careless wording would not justify.

Our Opportunity*

1863, November 9

A careful collection of reports from different well-informed quarters shows the entire strength of the Rebel army on this side of the Mississippi (that is of all that is of any use) to be in round numbers as follows:

Bragg's Army 75,000

Lee's Army 40,000

Beauregard's Army 20,000

Johnston's Army (in the rear of
    Vicksburg and Memphis) 18,000
    At Wilmington 10,000
    At Mobile 6,000

Scattering 20,000

There are about 20,000 on the West side of the Mississippi (there were 40,000 three months ago), but their

*This "Agate" letter not in the Reid collection appeared in the *Gazette,* of November 12, 1863.

members are being rapidly diminished by desertions and at
any rate isolated as they are, they are utterly useless for
the sustenance of the Rebellion.

Practically then we are confronted today by not over
one hundred and ninety thousand men. We can meet them
with an effective *mobile* of at the very least three hundred
and fifty thousand.

Is there any reason that a people unwilling to prolong
needless slaughter for the sake of affording high positions
to military men will be willing to accept, why—if the
General-in-Chief wants it—the war cannot be ended by
Christmas? Can any possible reason be conceived why it
should under the most adverse circumstances imaginable
be prolonged after next 4th of July.

If we look beyond the mere numbers of the armies in
the field, the comparison between the Rebel situation and
our own is still more in our favor.

We are about to reinforce our armies with "three hundred thousand more" either by volunteering or by the
draft. No sane man will doubt that in one way or the other
we will get them. In their army the conscriptions do not
supply the drain of the desertions; and their whole arms
bearing population has already been called out.

We hold the vantage ground at Chattanooga (which is
really today the battleground of the Rebellion); we hem
them in as by a wall of fire by our gunboats on the
Mississippi and our iron clads along the coast; we have cut
them off from their two great sources of supplies—East
Tennessee with the rich countries to which it was the gate
and Texas; and we have deprived them of half the territory
through which they hoped to be able to enforce their
conscription act.

Our finances are on as sound a basis as ever; theirs have

reached such as pass that, in the very midst of their thickening disasters by land and sea, at home and abroad, they pronounce the care of their currency more vital even than the care of their armies.

We are no longer menaced by British intervention; and we need hardly anticipate that of France alone. They have lost their last hope of active aid from any European power, their cotton loan is virtually retired from the market, their envoy retires in disgust from the British court, and their rams are seized in British waters.

And the last fear of trouble at home is dispelled. The People—when did they ever fail?—have come magnificently up to the support of the Government; have given it the control of Congress, have poured out their treasure at its feet, have borne one draft and stand saying, "draft again, if you need the men—only give us vigor and earnestness in prosecuting the war to the end."

In one word the game of the Rebellion has reached its last stage, and we hold all the points in our hands. Shall we throw them away? Or, shall we not hold to a stern responsibility those military authorities who, already needing forgiveness for much in the Past, may still persist in frittering away our opportunities?

The President at Gettysburg

1863, November 19

The President has gone to Gettysburg today. Singularly enough, the only Cabinet members who found time to accompany him were the Conservative ones, Seward, Blair, Bates and Usher. The Radicals, Chase, Welles and Stanton, are hard at work in their Departments. The accuracy with which chance thus followed the line of political distinction attracts some attention. It was mentioned to bluff and hearty, U. S. Treasurer Spinner, this evening at the dinner table, "Nobody but the Conservatives went up to Gettysburg with the President." "There's d____d good Scripture for that," gruffly responded the General, "*Let the dead bury the dead.*" It is hoped Messrs. Seward and Blair won't think this personal.

The Chase Movement*

1864, February 26

The public mind, or at least the newspaper mind, seems to have been considerably bewildered by some of the late moves and checks and supposed checkmates in the Presidential game now playing—to the great dissatisfaction of most disinterested men, who agree with Senator John Conness that it is a time to make war rather than Presidents—on the national chess board.

Perhaps the most amusing evidence of this bewilderment is the mistake some prominent newspapers have fallen

---

* This "Agate" letter not in the Reid collection appeared in the *Gazette* of February 29, 1864.

into, that the action of the National Committee in fixing the Administration Convention at Baltimore on the 7th of June is a part of what they call the "Chase movement." It was, on the contrary, the most emphatic reverse the "Chase movement" has encountered.

The public at large hoped for as long a postponement of the Convention as possible that the Presidential campaign might not distract that of our armies. It happened that the Chase managers, as they are called (and for that matter, the Butler managers, the Fremont managers, the Banks managers, and the rest) supposed . . . [that it would be] in their interest too, as well as that of the Nation, in putting off the Convention. "If it comes soon," they argued, "the present feeling for Mr. Lincoln will sweep everything before it." "If it should be postponed there are all the chances delay may offer for the advancement of our men and the abatement of the Lincoln enthusiasm." And so they fell in with the popular desire and did their best to put off the Convention till late summer or early autumn.

When the National Committee met, then, at Governor Edwin D. Morgan's residence the other day it at once resolved itself into two parties. The Lincoln party wanted an early Convention to reap the harvest while it was ripe. The others wanted a late Convention to give time for changes and accidents.

The contest began by a proposition from a Lincoln man that the Convention should meet *in May*. This was strenuously advocated on the ground that whatever struggle there was to be could come in the Convention; that the nomination would be equivalent to the election; and that, therefore, the sooner it was over the sooner the people would be ready to give their united attention to the war.

The friends of all the other positive and possible candidates insisted that the issue was not so sure but that a united attention to the war *beforehand,* through the spring and summer, would make it sure and less dangerous to the well being of the country.

Finally, however, there seemed to be danger that May would be finally selected as the month for holding the Convention, one of the opposition members proposed June and asked that a vote be taken between the two months. It was agreed to, and the Chase, Butler, etc., wing carried by one or two majority. The struggle then came over the time of the month. The successful party proposed the 28th, the others the 7th, and this time the Lincoln side won by a small majority, and the 7th of June was fixed upon as the day. At the outset the "Chase managers," acting on what was manifestly their best policy, proposed to delay the Convention till August, and it is even understood that an early day in September was mentioned. . . .

The only important question in the warfare of the Blairs and their allies on Mr. Chase, intended to drive him from the Cabinet, is whether Mr. Lincoln in the remotest degree approves or countenances it. The moment it appears that he does or that there is reasonable suspicion that he does, the portfolio of the Treasury Department will be for the third time within a year once more placed at his disposal. It is not generally known, I believe, but it is true, that some months after the Cabinet had gone through the Senatorial attack when Mr. Seward and Mr. Chase both tendered their resignations, Mr. Chase felt compelled again to address a note to Mr. Lincoln unconditionally resigning his position. Mr. Lincoln refused it, and it is only now by virtue of that refusal that Mr. Chase is now in the Cabinet at all. His own choice was to retire.

Grant and the 1864 Campaign

1864, April 28

There is a moral to be drawn from the opening of the campaign that should now of all times be inculcated. *We may fail.*

What then? Why, simply what we have had again and again before—we must begin anew. Everything is *not* staked on the approaching battle; all our hopes are *not* wrapped up in Lieutenant General Grant. A second Chancellorsville, a third Bull Run may be before us; confidence may be lost in Grant as before in McClellan, in Burnside, in Hooker; but whoever believes in God, *knows* what the end of the war is to be.

It is a time, then not for foolish assurance, but for patient, faithful hope. In spite of the successive disasters that have crowded upon one another through the opening campaign, there is here no discouragement. Three years have given us some steadiness under reverse, some self control under brightening prospects. We look to the gathering armies, the accumulating supplies, the cautious counselings we see from day to day with the confidence they rightfully inspire; but the day has passed when possible defeat can bring again the unmanly despair of the first Bull Run.

1864, May 23

The Recent Battles

There has been a not unnatural reaction in the public mind with the reference to the value of our successes in the Wilderness and at Spotsylvania Court House. The engagements are found to have been in the main protracted and hotly contested skirmishes, rather than great battles; and the number of killed and wounded conclusively shows that, instead of "equaling Solferino and Magenta," they rather resembled such affairs as the seven days' retreat on the Peninsula.

The contest may have been obstinately protracted, but a loss of twenty or even thirty thousand, in eight days' fighting, (and two-thirds of those so slightly wounded as scarcely to deserve being treated as disabled) does not indicate fighting like that of Gettysburg, or Pea Ridge, or Pittsburg Landing.

"Changing His Base" as a System

The latest movement develops a novel feature in the campaign. The great difficulty hitherto in our aggressive operations has been the difficulty of keeping open our line of communications as we advanced farther and farther from our base into the rebel territory. In the West this difficulty has once or twice thrown us back toward the Ohio River; in the East though the lines are vastly shorter it has almost invariably been regarded insurmountable.

General Grant, as is now seen, has adopted the novel

policy of throwing forward his base from point to point
and opening successive new lines of communication as he
advances. By moving toward Richmond on a line crossing
the numerous rivers on the route near their respective
heads of navigation, he need not at any time be more than
from ten to twenty miles distant from water communication, patrolled by our gunboats, and affording an easy road
to Washington, which the rebels can neither tear up nor
blockade by burning its bridges. Guerillas and raiding cavalry parties can do no harm to the Rappahannock, the
Mattapony, or the Pamunky.

When Grant moved from Brandy Station, he refused to
attack the rebels in their works at the Mine Run and
preferred to turn their flank. There was at once imminent
danger of their falling upon his line of communications as
he lengthened it out by the very side of their army. To
avoid this he abandoned the line entirely, and when presently he was ready to open one, he directed it, not northwest toward his old position at Brandy Station, but northeast in the rear of his new position to Fredericksburg and
Acquia Creek. On the Potomac we were, of course, by the
aid of our gunboats supreme. We had therefore a line of
barely twenty miles, and that almost inaccessible to the
enemy, to guard.

Lee having again established himself in intrenched works
at Spotsylvania, Grant once more turns his right by a
sudden march on Bowling Green. That would again expose
his line of communications; but he at once throws forward
his base from Fredericksburg with its connection by rail
with the Potomac to Port Royal (but a few miles from
Bowling Green) with its direct water connections with the

Bay. This new base is once more in the rear of the army in its new position; and is removed as far as possible, from exposure to the enemy.

In this statement seems to be the whole of Grant's strategy for his new campaign against Richmond. If the rebels come in his way and he can't get around them, he fights; but if possible, he turns the flank of their intrenched positions, and throws his own base forward, as he does it to another and still another new line of water communication with Richmond. The army is thus left free to devote its whole strength to the contest with Lee; while the navy is required to do the main work of guarding the supplies and keeping open the line of communications.

Fredericksburg is already abandoned. The wounded have been hurried off by boat and rail to Washington; the last supply trains have been sent down the Richmond road to Bowling Green; and the crowd of visitors, Sanitary and Christian Commission agents, nurses and anxious relatives, have made haste to get away. In a day or two Fredericksburg will be as Brandy and Rappahannock Stations are while the last new base, Port Royal, is already populous with boats and wagons and the busy swarm of attendants on the movements of a great army—only to have its brief season of bustle and uproar, to be in turn deserted.

1864, May 24

About the Strategy at Spotsylvania

The dispute which has raged for a day or two as to whether Grant maneuvered Lee out of his position at Spotsylvania Court House, or whether Lee deceived Grant

into believing he was still there in strength by a show of
force, while he had really stolen away with the bulk of his
army and made good his retreat, seemes settled this morning by a cautious expression of the official bulletin. Mr.
Stanton admits that Lee started first and was well on his
way before Grant began his flanking operation. We may as
well acknowledge, therefore, that Lee got the better of us.

It does not follow, however, that he was not substantially driven away by Grant's policy. He must have seen
from the outset that his position was untenable the moment Grant chose to march past him at Bowling Green,
and he may have hoped by retreating to induce Grant to
follow directly on his track, and so lengthen out the line of
communications and give him a chance to cut it. If he had
any such view in hastening his movement, he was disappointed. Grant's line of communications is as safe now
as it was when he suddenly threw his base across from
Brandy Station to Fredericksburg.

Whoever supposes now that because Lee has retreated
and we are twenty miles nearer Richmond, the contest is
substantially over, is once more foolishly allowing his
hopes to run away with his judgment. Lee's army is still a
compact, splendidly-disciplined body. It is operating on
the defensive and in the main behind fortifications; and
this to a great extent counterbalances the disparity of
numbers. It fights with the desperation of men defending
not merely their homes, but the city which is the very seat
and symbol of their "Government"; and even if it *has* been
convinced that its cause is hopeless, the energy of a brave
man's despair is a terrible thing to meet. Of course we shall
win—no one doubts that—but there is hard fighting still
ahead of us.

1864, June 14

Grant's Greatness

I have never been intoxicated with admiration for General Grant; but he has always seemed to possess two elements of genuine greatness.

On the evening of the first day at Pittsburg Landing, everybody was despondent. We had been taken at a disadvantage and driven back in confusion; line after line had been shattered, division after division had given up its tale of killed and wounded and seen its quota of prisoners carried off to fill the rebel prisons; thousands of our men slunk beneath the river bluffs, a coward mob; the rest had been driven from point to point, till at last a bare half mile from the river bank, naught but one single semi-circle of hastily mounted guns stood between the remnants of our army and sheer destruction. In front was the splendid army of the rebels, flushed with victory, and pressing forward to complete its work; behind was the river. General Grant and his staff gathered in a little group by the post office. Said one to him, "General, the prospect looks a little bad." "Oh, no, not at all," he quietly replied; "we can stand it out tonight; in the morning we'll have fresh men, and they won't; of course we'll whip them, sir."

"Of course we'll whip them, sir." *There* was one element of greatness. He didn't know what it was to be discouraged. And another, not less marked, and in those times, even more valuable than it is now, was his splendid pugnacity. In the days when McClellan exalted Manassas and Buell talked of strategy before Bowling Green; when everywhere a man was held in estimation according as he showed reasons for not fighting, General Grant stood a special exception to the rule. He was always ready to fight, and he never knew when he was whipped.

Can we not now add a third element of military greatness? Does not his movement from the Chickahominy to the south side of the James prove him as willing to change his plans for better ones, as he has been found obstinate in sticking to the best?

"I have lost a great battle, solely through my own fault," said Frederick the Great once. It proved him worthy of his title. Only great men can afford to admit mistakes or to change their plans in the face of criticism. If General Grant had been a small man, he would have tried to fight it out on the north side of Richmond. The most encouraging sign in his whole campaign is this abandonment of that policy and the movement to the south of the James.

The Republican Convention

1864, June 7
From Baltimore

A morning of caucuses and button-holing manifold; of electioneering for the Vice-Presidency and wire-pulling for the Chairmanship of the Convention; of jostling crowds in the hotels, innumerable mint juleps in the private parlors, and convocations at the several State headquarters; of speculations over the Missouri question; of denunciations of the Cabinet; of hurrying arrivals, salutations, hand-shaking, blarney, wisky-guzzling, and confused inquiries of the Baltimore rebels for the locality of the Front Street Theatre; and so, after much rushing about and fast talking and hard working, a great mass of sweaty, cozy humanity is packed into the Hall, where, four years ago, STEPHEN A. DOUGLAS was nominated for the Presidency. By what strange happening it is that another son of Illinois, *his* friend and rival, should now receive a higher honor in the same place.

There is none of the shouting and mad cheering and wild enthusiasm which we are accustomed to associate with National Conventions. An ordinary Ohio Convention would furnish quite as much enthusiasm.

Looking over the mass of delegates on the floor, one is surprised to see so few well known faces. To the left of the platform the surly features beneath the almost historic wig of Thaddeus Stevens are noticeable. By the side of the caustic old Leader of the House is the spare form of the Ex-Secretary of War with the sharp, sallow face and the sparse gray hair, so well known in Pennsylvania wherever Legislatures are to be bought or offices to be disposed of [*sic*.]. Four years ago, this Simon Cameron was among the most prominent rivals of Mr. Seward and Mr. Lincoln for the Presidency; now he has been anxious to take the second place on the ticket with his successful homespun competitor.

One fails to find many other notable people visible from the platform. Directly in front in the midst of the delegation are the two latest Governors of Ohio, one of them the destined Chairman of the Convention. Across the aisle, and but a few feet from them, sits the editorial leader of the distinctive Lincoln movement in the Union party, Gov-

ernor Henry J. Raymond of the New York *Times.* How
names stick! Long ago Horace Greeley petulantly called
him the "Little Villain," and you can hear in half a dozen
quarters the whispered remark, "that's the Little Villain
from New York over there." The Little Villain is smart,
and looks it—compact, keen, practical-looking, with a
sparkling, restless eye, as unlike Mr. Greeley as it is possible for one man to be unlike another. He is to make his
mark in the Convention before it is ended. [Reid then
described a number of others at the convention.]

In a few moments the States are called and the list made
up.

The rebel States, however, give rise to a dispute. Thaddeus Stevens objects to calling them. Horace Maynard
insists, pleads the case of Tennessee, and at last, through
the sympathies he arouses, carries the case. I need say
nothing of the debate. It is simply a passage from the
familiar House debates, transferred to this new arena. It is
very sharp, and animated; but it is all very old.

The rebel States and the territories are finally called;
and their credentials referred to a committee. It is a
dangerous precedent; and it opens the way for worse that
yet remains behind.

There is a rush of routine business, appointment of
committees and the like, and the Convention takes a
recess.

In the evening, the permanent organization is effected;
Governor Dennison [of Ohio] makes a patriotic little
speech on taking the chair; Parson Brownlow says some of
his old things to this new audience and nominates Andy
Johnson for Vice President; and so the Convention ad-
journs. I do the same.

June 8

The Convention is over. Its nominations have been completed—its platform has been adopted—the little efforts at
notoriety for the sake of getting offices hereafter have all
been made; and as the delegates are all seizing their carpet-
bags and rushing for the trains, I begin to write some
matters which the telegraph may have left for me to
say. . . .

By breakfast time this morning matters had settled
down into this shape: The Radicals were to be admitted
[after a protracted debate in the Credentials Committee],
Johnson was to be vigorously pressed for the Vice-Presidency, and an effort was to be made to get in the rebel
State vote and that of the Territories to help him through.
Pennsylvania's fifty-two votes gave solidity to Mr. Hamlin's
candidacy. The War Democratic element pressed Dickinson. No others were serious candidates and on no other
questions was any division expected.

Long before nine o'clock a crowd assembled outside the
door of the theater in which the Convention assembled. By
ten every part of the building was packed; but there was
comparatively little excitement. "This Convention hasn't
the enthusiasm of a decent town meeting," growled an
Illinois delegate. He was to see before long that it could at
any rate make plenty of noise. . . .

The Missouri Radicals

At last the immense, dumpy, flour-barrel form of Preston King waddled out in front of the chair, and the
ex-Senator began the report of the Committee on Creden-

tials. This was the signal for the opening of the real struggle. It was more one-sided than was expected.

A fearful parliamentary tangle first tied up the whole question, and nobody who could was found to untie it. The storm of questions and demands for the question and risings to questions of order and statements of questions of privilege, shouts and clamor, applause and hisses, raged for a long time. At last the knot was in some mysterious way sliced in two—though I hear Schuyler Colfax or Solomon Foote would have been very much puzzled to tell how— and two or three five-minute speeches on the merits of the case were got in. Brandegee, of Connecticut—member of the House and thoroughly "sharp" laywer—secured the attention of the crowd and pithily stated the facts as developed before the committee. Dr. Breckinridge sweepingly denied everything Brandegee had said, denounced the radicals and avowed his readiness to prove before any jury that all their claims were false. George William Curtis briefly and elegantly pleaded the cause of the radicals and carried the Convention with him; and Mr. Delano got out, inspite of the rule, some important facts about the comparative unamimity of the Committee's action.

Then came another stormy scene to settle how the vote should be taken and on what. Dr. Breckinridge's motion that the radicals and conservatives divide the vote between them was shouted down by a storm of noes. Preston King's motion that both be admitted and that when they couldn't agree neither should vote, met a similar fate. Dr. Breckinridge by magnificent pluck forced the Convention to hear him make a speech on it, but the speech gained him nothing.

At last the vote by States on the proposition to admit

the radicals only was reached. Everybody knows the result. Three postmasters in Pennsylvania and Dr. Breckinridge voted for Frank Blair's bogus conservative delegates, and that was absolutely their whole muster of strength in the entire Union party! It stood four hundred and forty to four. The four doubtless thought the four hundred and forty very obstinate and unreasonable men!

It was a superb radical triumph. They had expected to be admitted, for they knew it to be their right; but that the abused, proscribed, disowned radicals of Missouri should sweep this Lincoln Convention with a broom that only missed—three Pennsylvania postmasters and a Kentuckian, who, as his own words happily express it, has always been in a party to himself—was a victory as splendid as it was unexpected. Of course the reason is manifest. The German radicals had to be conciliated. We couldn't afford to lose Missouri; and besides Southern Illinois depended largely on Missouri's course. The inevitable nomination of Mr. Lincoln would be displeasing to the radical elements interested in the Missouri case; this decision was an effort to conciliate them in advance. The policy was good, the decision was just, and the majority of the Union party heartily believed it so; but it would have been more gratifying if motives like those just named had not so palpably influenced the action of others.

Admission of Rebel States

Then came the lamentable feature of the Convention. That irrepressible demagogue, General Jim Lane, had evidently prepared a programme of action, which he deemed important enough to be persistently and vehemently pushed. It is plain now, that from the outset, he and certain others having their own ends to accomplish thereby had determined to perpetrate the outrage of bringing into the Convention on an equal footing with Ohio or Indiana States that could cast no electoral vote, territories that had no more voice in the Presidential election than Ireland or Denmark could have, and rebel States absolutely unorganized and having no government save that of the rebels or of the army.

At first the demand was moderate. It was only asked that Tennessee should be allowed to vote. The sufferings of the noble East Tennesseeans, the gallantry of the State, the fame of Andrew Johnson, all combined to make every delegate wish to give them what they asked. Horace Maynard spoke handsomely of their claims; everybody's sympathies were with them; and so by virtue of their general good character they carried their point. . . .

The galleries . . . were with the Tennesseeans. So were the wishes of the delegates. Ohio had in the morning voted in caucus to go for Andrew Johnson for Vice President. She could hardly, therefore, vote to keep Andrew Johnson's delegates out. Her vote changed the scale. Forty-two votes thrown solid made their mark. The majority was 52 against the admission, but the delegates didn't so understand it, and the excitement over Ohio's solid ballot led them to suppose either that Tennessee was admitted or that the vote was exceedingly close. Thereupon the weak-kneed gave way, a few changes were made, the majority was turned, and the wedge was well entered. How far it forced its way was soon seen.

"Tennessee is unorganized" shouts Jim Lane, the moment the tumultuous applause over her admission dies out.

"You have admitted her; how can you deny admission to organized States like Louisiana and Arkansas?" That shows the hand. How may you, indeed? The precedent has been set; where will it not lead you?

What follows may be foreseen. The Convention cannot turn round and stultify itself on such short notice; accordingly it admits Louisiana and Arkansas. Colorado, Nevada, and Nebraska are at least as good as these rebel States and in *they* come. It were as well to bring in minors in a county convention to name the candidates even though they can't next week cast their ballots for the very candidates they have chosen! But it is done. There was a small precedent for it at Chicago; but nobody expected such consequences. Even yet the end of its legitimate results has not been reached.

The platform comes next. Raymond reads it so that everybody can hear, and the applause that storms about the closing words of every resolution is enough to show that those who hear are satisfied. But there are two things in the reading especially noteworthy. The resolution for the abolition of slavery everywhere evokes the wildest and most enthusiastic applause. And next to that comes the protest against French interference in Mexico.

Nomination of Mr. Lincoln

Next follows a curious scene of small ambition. The Convention is ready for nominations. Columbus Delano nominates Mr. Lincoln. In an instant Simon Cameron, old wire-puller that he is, is on his feet. He has a resolution, towit: That Lincoln and Hamlin be renominated by acclamation! For a moment it startles the Convention into

silence. Then a storm of noes comes up. Members appeal
to Cameron to withdraw. The sturdy Scotchman shakes his
head and holds his ground. He wants, he says, to see them
show their hands. . . .

Violent opposition has been manifested to the obviously
just connection of Hamlin's name with that of Lincoln (I
say obviously just, for I cannot conceive of any reason for
Mr. Lincoln's renomination that will not operate as an
implied censure upon Mr. Hamlin, provided he also be *not*
renominated), such opposition has been made to it that
Mr. Cameron has finally consented to let the vote be taken
first on Lincoln alone. . . .

At last the call of the States begins. It goes as everybody
expects—all voting for Mr. Lincoln, and no little enthusiasm being displayed at every mention of the name till
Missouri is reached. Mr. Hume, of the St. Louis *Democrat*,
takes the floor; briefly and handsomely states that under
instruction they cannot on the first ballot vote for Mr.
Lincoln, and casts the vote of the State for—Ulysses S.
Grant!

There is no confusion or clamor; but there runs around
the hall a peculiar buzz—"sensation," the papers call it.
That is a new play not looked for in the game. It can't win;
but may it bring any complications for the future with it?
Suppose the Chicago Convention, for instance, should
nominate General Grant; what about Missouri? . . .

At last the call is ended, and the Chairman announces
that Mr. Lincoln has all the votes but those of Missouri;
and Mr. Hume is again on his feet. He moves that the
nomination of Abraham Lincoln be made unanimous, and
the happy motion, coming from exactly the right quarter,
goes through with a perfect whirlwind of applause. . . .

The Vice-Presidency

The real fight then opened. An Indianian nominated Andrew Johnson of Tennessee for the Vice-Presidency, and the Johnson men cheered. . . . Lyman Tremain nominated and praised Daniel S. Dickinson, and the Dickinson men cheered quite as loud as the Johnson men had done a moment ago. Simon Cameron in a quiet, business like way nominated Hannibal Hamlin, but the cheers were feeble. For some reason or other it was plain that Mr. Hamlin had lost his hold. Men seemed to consider it their duty to support him; but there was no enthusiasm about it.

At last the confusion quieted, and the balloting began; each side cheering lustily the votes its candidates received. It was evident that no one had a majority. Two or three States scattered their votes, but of the three real candidates, Johnson was only a little ahead. The rebel States, just admitted, voted for him; so did the Territories, and it was by this aid that he was foremost.

But no matter how he gained the plurality, he has it, and the impression spreads among the delegates that it is almost if not quite a majority. A few slight changes are made in his favor—not nearly enough to nominate him; but it is believed that they are. Thereupon Cameron rises, tired of working for Hamlin, whom his own section is so slow to support, and changes the fifty-two votes of Pennsylvania to Andrew Johnson! That settles it, and the storm of applause renders it utterly impossible for Thaddeus Stevens to make himself heard in his efforts to protest that Pennsylvania was *not* ready thus to change. The clamor overbore him; and a rush to change and be on the winning side went on till Dickinson and Hamlin had scarcely a corporal's guard apiece; and Johnson's nomination was well nigh unanimous. It was at once made wholly so; and the work of the Convention was substantially done.

June 9

The nomination of Mr. Johnson for the Vice-Presidency marks a triumph of a policy in the Convention diametrically opposite to that resolved upon by the Union members of Congress. The admission of the rebel States and the territories to vote on precisely the same footing with States like New York and Ohio was part of the same general movement and was evidently contrived by the same head.

After all, however, it was mainly accident that gave Mr. Johnson the nomination. No choice was expected on the first ballot. Indiana had agreed to turn on the second ballot her twenty-six votes solid for Hamlin. Other changes would have been made, and Johnson's showing would not have been so good as on the first ballot. At the end of the call the vote stood, Johnson, 198, Hamlin, 150, Dickinson, 110, the rest scattering. Of this plurality of 48, not less than 42 came from the territories and the rebel States. The general impression, however, was that he had nearly or quite a majority, and under this the changes began.

Every effort was made by the New Yorkers to secure a nomination as soon as possible in order to defeat Dickinson. It was openly declared by the Weed men in the New York caucus that the nomination of Dickinson was equivalent to putting Mr. Seward out of the Cabinet; and this they were not willing under any circumstances to permit. When therefore, they found Johnson ahead, the Weed men at once threw their whole force for him.

A few men like Thaddeus Stevens perceived the complications that must spring from the nomination of a candidate from a region where no electoral vote could be cast;
but I think it true that a vast majority of the delegates
never thought of it. They admired Johnson's splendid
stand against secession, and wanted to reward him for it;
they sympathized with Tennessee, and wanted to show it;
and so the majority of the votes he got were cast without a
single thought of the awkward questions they were raising.

Nobody here objects personally to Johnson—there is
indeed the warmest admiration for him; but there were
grave doubts with many as to the constitutional question
involved; and others fear the influence of the nomination
on the system of bogus reconstruction so much in vogue.
"I am delighted," said Secretary Chase, when Johnson had
so manfully taken his stand in the Senate against secession,
"I am delighted to learn that Andrew Johnson is only the
modern way for spelling *Andrew Jackson*." It was not an
extravagant expression of the regard in which he has been
held.

Democrats

1864, August 26
From Chicago

In New York (as at Washington) I had found the feeling
of the Administration leaders not quite as hopeful as one
could wish. In Philadelphia it was the reverse. They were
altogether too hopeful to realize that hard work must be
done before we can, in brokers' parlance, discount the
profits on our coming campaign. At the Loyal League the

most absolute confidence seemed to reign. One or two croakers, returning like myself, from the seaside or from summer travel, told ugly stories about alleged disaffections in the Union ranks and danger of desertions to the compact, disciplined enemy; but they were pooh-poohed away. Philadelphia Unionists do not believe that any combination of circumstances or conjunction of planets can prevent Mr. Lincoln's reelection.

Our train westward contained parts of several eastern delegations to Chicago, and, after leaving Pittsburgh, squads of the un-delegate Democracy began to pour in on us at every station and flooded out all our established rights to comfortable seats.

Of course we had nothing but political talk all the way. Fortunately I was fortified with an old novel of Bulwer's and so had a refuge from the discussions. It was well, for they offered nothing new; and a very few sentences furnished the key notes. . . .

Two features of all this loose conversation were worthy of special notice. Every man talked, not boastingly, but as a matter of course with the perfect confidence of success; and every man refered gloatingly to our military failure as giving assurance of that success.

The first has not hitherto been sufficiently heeded. The Democrats manifestly expect to succeed this fall. Nor have they any fears of a serious split. No man can tell what next week may have in store for us; but there can now be seen no apprehension whatever of a rupture. The absolute unity of the party in supporting the candidate, whoever he may be, is hardly questioned by anybody; they seem to regard it as a thing beyond question. They are hungry for offices, they have their eyes very wide open to the effects of the Charleston rupture four years ago, they are in the thorough state of discipline that being thrown into the opposition always gives them, and they are going into this fight hoping and expecting to win. I do not believe they will, but I do know that we have a very good chance here to learn from our enemies!

But the saddest thing in all this political talk was the evident delight at our military failures. I do not write the words willingly; for, realizing profoundly that this rebellion can be put down by no party and by no effort that stops short of embracing the PEOPLE of the North, I know how fully it is admitting that the end of these troublous times is not yet in sight. But there could be no mistaking the tone of exultation in which the invasion of the North and the siege of the Capital in the fourth year of the war were paraded, and Grant's flanking operations were laughed at, and the ability of Jefferson Davis was exultantly eulogized. Let us only hope that in this, at least, they were no fair representatives of the constituencies that sent them to Chicago!

And so, while the rustic stump speaker bellows away at the luckless Republican who set him off, and the longer heads count up the delegations "sure for McClellan on the first ballot," I turn to my Bulwer, and find consolation.

1864, August 28

Any comparison of this with the Baltimore Convention is simply absurd. I have seen a dozen State Conventions as large and enthusiastic as this was. This I suppose to have no parallel in our political history, save its Republican predecessor of four years ago. At Baltimore there was no outside pressure. . . .

Respectability

It is, on the whole, a *cleaner*-looking Convention than we are used to find under the Democratic label. No one who is familiar with the unwashed elements, the hard-headed, raw boned old fellows from the rural districts, with shocky reddish hair and enormous tobacco quids, who tell you they have "always been Dimmycrats, them and their fathers before 'em;" the jolly fellows with great round corporations and sparkling noses, who look as if they had followed the liquor retailing business from their youth up in sound Democratic communities; the broad faced, genial looking men, of immense muscle, and immense stomach capacity, with big heads, well kept up by big bellies, with hearty ways and an off hand humor, who have been time out of mind the popular Democratic leaders, and of whom Douglas will always remain the conspicuous type—no one, I say, who is familiar with all these elements in our ordinary Democratic Convention will need to have the meaning of the saying explained, when it is observed that it is a cleaner-looking Convention than usual.

There are not many of the men here who always give character to large Administration meetings—no men of literary fame like George William Curtis; no great editors like Horace Greeley or Henry J. Raymond; no veterans like Thaddeus Stevens, whose abilities extort the respect his acts do not always command; but of the solid men of the country, successful business men, railroad kings, smart, popular advocates, shrewd lobbyists, in short of all the upper and better strata of the Democratic managers, there is an overwhelming supply. . . .

"It's time this thing was stopped. We've shed blood enough; and we've done as much wrong to the rebels as they've ever done to us. Now let's stop it." That is the most common sentiment we hear.

"We won't stand another draft. Lincoln's afraid to draft before the election, and after that he can't." This recurs almost as often.

"Guess they've got about enough of it by this time. They were going to do great things when they got Grant; but old Lee's been too smart for him too, and he's been splendidly beaten every time he showed fight. We've spent a hundred thousand lives in getting back to the point they made McClellan leave two years ago." Thus many more.

"Beat them? Of course we will! Thousand of thousands of Republicans are going to vote with us. Nothing but a splendid victory can give them a ghost of a chance, and we needn't have any fear about their winning victories. That's a thing that isn't in their line." Thus many others.

Among them all there is this perfect confidence in success. . . .

"I'd much rather make a fair, out and out fight on an avowed peace man [such as Vallandingham], if I thought we could afford it," is a remark one hears at every corner. "But I suppose," they always add, "that McClellan is a more available man."

Sheridan

1864, October 21

The ruddy glow of these warm and ripe October days matches well with the fruitage our Battle-Autumn is bringing us. The grip on Petersburg and Richmond unrelaxed; the desperate effort of Hood in the southwest nervelessly lapsing into an effort to escape from the pursuing legions he had hoped to throw back to Nashville, if not to the Ohio; and last and crowning glory of the month, a victory in the Valley that, if not in far reaching results, at least in tenacity of fighting and splendor of success wrested from the jaws of defeat, may be worthily named after Marengo—such is a brief and true epitome of the situation.

Some portions of the recent movements in the Valley belong, as yet, to unwritten history. Everybody watched Sheridan's brilliant course up the Shenandoah from Harper's Ferry to Winchester, from Winchester to Opequan, from Opequan to Fisher's Hill, from Fisher's Hill to Harrisonburg and Staunton, from Staunton to Rockfish Gap. Then came a sudden blank, broken only by indistinct rumors of uncomprehended cavalry skirmishes, and ended, to everybody's half concealed surprise, by a sudden "retiring" to Strasburg.

Why the blank? Why the retreat? The rebel journals give hints; but it is to private intelligence we must trust for the full explanation.

The campaign in the Shenandoah Valley was complete in itself when Early's army was beaten and broken, the Valley cleared, and the standing menace to the Border removed. It remained to utilize these local successes for Grant and for the armies before Richmond. This might be attempted in two ways: by a movement on Lynchburg, taking the stores and workshops and cutting the leading artery of Richmond supply; or by a movement on Charlottesville or Gordonsville, that would plant this victorious army of the Valley on the west flank—so to speak—of

Richmond and within cooperating distance of Butler and
Meade.

The first was decided to be so difficult as to be almost
impracticable; and it was doubted if the advantages would
pay the cost. Lynchburg was known to be well defended
and it was nearly sixty miles still further south from
Staunton; while Sheridan's line of communications was
already lengthened out through a guerilla infested country
and without railroads for a distance of a hundred and
twenty miles. Lynchburg was therefore abandoned.

Charlottsville, however, seemed accessible; and the
whole time intervening between Sheridan's arrival at
Staunton and the sudden retiring to Strasburg was spent in
efforts to open a way through the mountains to it. The
direct road from Staunton to Charlottsville led through
Rockfish Gap, and that was first tried. The Gap was found
to be strongly defended by Early's men so that a passage
was impracticable. After severe skirmishing we gave it up.
The others were then tried in succession. Jourdan's Gap,
Brown's Gap, Semon's, and Swift Run Gap, each was
found strongly guarded by a rebel force that could not be
dislodged short of siege approaches or the cutting of new
roads over mountains that have always been considered
impassable. At most of them there was sharp skirmishing;
at some, it is said, tolerably heavy fighting.

At any rate, the upshot of it all was that the movement
on Charlottsville had to be abandoned. It remained to
bring back the army to Strasburg which is the natural gate
to the Valley, establish a chain of strong military posts
there, completely barring the way, and fortifying the gaps
along the Blue Ridge from Harper's Ferry down to Stras-

burg; and then to accomplish the cooperation which so large an army owed to the general development of the campaign in some other way.

But meantime, Early's scattered forces had been gathered together, Longstreet (as has been believed) had been sent up to them with heavy reenforcements; and so, the battle over which the rejoicings are still sounding through the Land.

How Sheridan Tells His Story

Sheridan's dispatches concerning this battle are to be taken precisely at their face value. Here at the Capital, where Western Generals are habitually subjected to unsparing criticism, it has been asked of late whether Sheridan did not sometimes recount his victories after the style of John Pope. The sneer is unjust as to Pope, but cruel as to Sheridan; for if ever there was a modest little hero, it is this same General Sheridan. The old remark about him at Rosecrans' headquarters used to be that "Sheridan writes his official dispatches, and even his indorsement on papers, precisely as he would tell what he thinks about the subject to an intimate friend." After all, isn't he right? For are not all of us, from one end of the country to the other, fast becoming firm friends of the hero of the Shenandoah?

The Parallel to Marengo and the Difference From It

Everybody has been comparing the late battle to Marengo, and, indeed, the points of similarity are striking enough. Marengo was at first a defeat—so was Cedar Creek;

the Austrians attacked early in the morning at Marengo—
the rebels did the same at Cedar Creek; Napoleon did not
arrive on the field till about 11—Sheridan perhaps an hour
later; at the arrival of their commanders the armies, French
and American alike rallied; there followed with each a
period of doubtful but steadying resistance to the enemy's
onset; at four Napoleon ordered the attack that cost him
Dessaix and won him the day. Sheridan was an hour
earlier; Napoleon swept the enemy into and through
Marengo, captured twenty pieces of artillery and eight
standards. Sheridan swept the enemy back beyond Fisher's
Hill, captured forty-three (or more) pieces of artillery and
ten standards. Napoleon's loss was 8,000; how much Sheridan's may be, widows and orphans all over the land must
sadly wait many weary days yet to know.

But there the parallel ends. Napoleon's victory was won
by the arrival of Dessaix's corps; Sheridan's was won by
the arrival of a General.

"I give you thirty thousand men to accomplish this
object," said the great General. "Sire, how do you reckon
up so many?" "The rolls show twenty thousand"; "I rate
you at ten thousand more!" It is the highest praise won by
a subordinate General in this war to say, as we can say of
Sheridan, that his single presence was worth on this doubtful field what Dessaix's whole corps was worth at Marengo.
All honor to the State [Ohio] that boasts such a General
among her contributions to the war.

Of the relations of this victory of the campaign before
Richmond it is too soon yet to speak. It is telling the
rebels, however, no more than the defeat of their force in
the Valley has already told them to say that it liberates for

Grant an army. Henceforth he may use it as to him seems best. Henceforth the fortifications now springing up about Strasburg are sufficient protection for the debatable land along the border.

The Effort and Failure in the Southwest

Meanwhile—to complete by a hasty glance at the Southwest, this survey of a military situation—the latest rebel movement against Sherman may be summed up in three sentences.

Hood attempted to repeat in 1864 the brilliant campaign of Bragg against Buell in 1862—to throw Sherman back from Atlanta to Chattanooga, from Chattanooga to Nashville, possibly even from Nashville to the Ohio, by moving steadily on his flank and threatening his line of communications as Bragg had done when he forced Buell back from Huntsville, Alabama, to Louisville. He attempted this, not with a large army, well fed, well provisioned, and moving on an inaccessible line from which it could debouch in our rear and retreat in safety again at pleasure; but with thirty thousand men, moving with only fifteen days' provisions, on a circuitous route, of which we held the interior lines. Passing Sherman's left flank, he struck his line of communications at Allatoona, was hastened away by Sherman's rapid approach on the shorter lines northward from Atlanta, moved up toward Chattanooga, found Thomas on his front and Sherman following fast on his rear, and gave it up.

Thenceforward his whole effort was to keep out of the way. He had reached Tunnel Hill, ten or fifteen miles from

Chattanooga; he was forced to turn sharp to the westward and make off to Lafayette and thence out through a difficult country into Alabama as fast as possible. If he succeeds in saving the remnants of his army, it will be the highest success the rebel authorities can hope for him. Sherman's hold upon Atlanta is as firm as ever; and Hood's spasmodic effort has only weakened and dispirited his army.

"Your feet shall press Tennessee soil," said Jefferson Davis. And again, "Hood has his eye on a point of the enemy's communications that will send him flying to the Ohio." Their feet did not press Tennessee soil; Sherman is doing pretty much the reverse of flying; and the disheartened army is hastening toward Montgomery. It has made its desperate effort that was to liberate the Gulf States and has failed.

The Lesson of It All

"Your only hope of peace, Mr. Davis, is in the ascendency of the Conservative party North. Fortify that party if you can by victory but do not neglect diplomacy." So, Honorable W. W. Boyce, of South Carolina, rebel Congressman, etc., etc., urges in a late letter to the rebel President. Apparently the rebel victory has not come to fortify the Conservative party aforesaid; it is consolatory to know that they can still resort to diplomacy. The rebel armies make no headway, but the rebel platform, proposing armistice and diplomacy is still in the field. Shall it be overwhelmed as utterly as Sheridan overwhelmed its ally at Cedar Creek?

Count Gurowski

1863, April 19

Meeting Count Gurowski (or Count Growler, as the wags want to call him) on the Avenue, half an hour ago, he burst out, "What a Government of asses! My Got, what a Government of asses, from Ass-in-Chief Halleck on down! Look at their opening of the campaign! See how they're already throwing away their powers! No brains, no plans— all blind asses, asses! Here's Halleck, who wouldn't be thought qualified to command a brigade, in the army of any respectable European Government—without ever having won a victory or even fought a battle, made General-in-Chief! Look at this brilliant book by Emil Schalk! Look how he predicted our disasters two years ago and how his predictions were fulfilled to the letter, and then look at what he says of our present movements! And *that* man you don't want in your service! I took him to them at the beginning of this war; I told who he was, what he had been; showed his work, and vat you think they offered him? A capitancy a capitancy of infantry! My Got! Halleck General-in-chief, and Emil Schalk offered a capitancy of infantry!" And with finger to his nose, and mouth working savagely under his gray beard, the irate Pole stumped off.

1863, October 22

"Ach, mein Gott, you Americans are a great people," storms Count Gurowski at the door; and the noble Pole's objurations come in appositely. "You forgot everyding. Your bress is in-famous. Your editors are cowards or scoundrels; and for my part I dink de scoundrels a little de best. Your *Herald* is a scoundrel. You accept that *a priori* ven you begin to read him; but your *Tribune* and your *Times,* and your *Post*—oh, faugh! Your leaders is cowards and im-be-ciles. De only ding I like in dis country is de great, noble, nameless masses, dat bear de load of all your stubidies, and fight your battles, and keep up your currency, and carry on your war, not because dey have any con-vi-dence in you, but because dey have con-vi-dence in demselves in spite of you."

"But down de losses on your side," continues the Count, "at four hundred thousand lives. One hundred thousand of dose lives I charge directly to de vac-il-ating policy of Seward, whom Lincoln *vill* keep in office; one hundred thousand to McClellan's policy, whom Lincoln *vould* keep in office; one hundred thousand directly to Lincoln's own half-handed vay of doing everyding. And yet, oh in-va-my, you elect him Bresident again, because he's hones, or else you elect Chase, because he brints greenbacks and dis great people is willing to dake dem. Vy don't you elect your bair of old breeches Bresident at once?"

It will be seen that the Count distributes his censures quite impartially. The second volume of his *Diary* is now in press, and is shortly to be issued by Carleton of New York. The first, it is understood, was sweet milk, compared with this one.

1865, March 18

The Supressed Volume

The old Count has been unusually quiet of late; but the secret is out. The last volume of his *Diary,* it seems, was so savage that he was either afraid to bring it out in this country, or unable to find an American publisher for it. He has accordingly had a few copies printed for private circulation, and has meanwhile actually sent the volume over to England for publication! I have been looking over the copy printed here—the Count having been kind enough to bring it in to show me how roundly he had abused the Press! It was characteristic of him; and to do him justice, he *has* berated us in good set terms, which even Bennett couldn't equal.

It is especially savage on Seward, whom it declares to have been the *murderer* of Wadsworth! The Presidential nomination at Baltimore greatly excited the old gentleman, and his pages about that date bristle with hard words that are almost as troublesome to swallow as the nomination was. Congress he is inclined to defend; and, *mirabile dictu,* he is in love with Governor Fenton, while he even speaks well of Governor Andrew and for the most part of Secretary Stanton. The book is dedicated to the memory of General James Wadsworth. It has been put under the charge in England of the eminent author John Stuart Mill—an old friend of Gurowski's by whom I more than half suspect it will be quietly smothered.

(I devoutly pray the Count may never see this paragraph. If he should, Washington will be too hot to hold me!)

I beg pardon, however, for referring to John Stuart Mill

just now as one of Gurowski's friends. "Vriend," exclaimed the old Count, a moment ago while his one eye glared ferociously on me, "Vriend—bah! I am no man's vriend" (The which I solemnly vouch for.) "Vriend! I abuse my best vriend tomorrow, if I dink he deserve it! Vriend—I don't know vat friendship is. *Do you dake me for a voman?*"

Yet, peace to the wrathful, unquiet old man! Liberty has had in this generation and land no sincerer, more self-sacrificing worshipper.

The Election

1864, November 11

In 1852 the Whig Party expired in the throes of a National defeat. Its great rival survived twelve years longer, only to dissolve at last in the same way. What the defeat of Winfield Scott was to the Whig Party, the defeat of George G. McClellan is to the Democratic. The one struggled afterward for years to maintain a show of existence in isolated localities; the other may very probably do the same. But the National defeat was the end of National vitality with the first, and so it will be with the second. The wrigglings of the Copperhead's tail prove, not its continued hold on life, but only the venmous fury with which it gives it up. . . .

Each was led to its defeat by a military man. . . .

I have said the last Tuesday wrought the death of the Democratic party. It wrought the death of something more important—SLAVERY! *That* is the true significance of our triumph. . . .

The election decides another thing. This people . . . have decreed that at whatever further cost, the republic shall be undivided and undivisible! . . .

These things were not passed upon and irreversibly settled by the people inconsiderately. There never was a political campaign in this country so free from mere partisan excitement and unbiassed by personal considerations. There was no personal enthusiasm; men voted for the cause and not for Mr. Lincoln. There was no partisan desire to sustain the course of the party—three-fourths of the leading speakers at the meetings could not have been induced to give the Administration their indorsement. But there was a determination, felt at every fireside, breathed in every meeting, infused into every ballot, that the Republic should stand, and its enemies should perish. It was the calm conclusion of the people, made after full trial of the cost, made under full pressure of the pain, made with a full determination to pay the cost and endure the pain, even to the end. The heroism of our countless battlefields has been glorious; but the heroism of the American People at the ballot box last Tuesday was sublime.

Lincoln's Plea for an Anti-Slavery Amendment

1864, December 6

The Message is of course in everybody's mouth. It is beyond a doubt the most popular of Mr. Lincoln's State

papers. His Emancipation Proclamation was looked upon
doubtingly by some and with bitter disapprobation by
others. His message two years ago with its astounding
scheme of gradual compensated emancipation to be
wrought out some time after the year 1900 was ignored by
Congress and gently laughed at by everybody. His Am-
nesty and Reconstruction policy of last year awoke bitter
opposition in the very heart of his party.

But the Message of today has at the first reading united
in approbation and admiration all wings and divisions of
Unionists. It presents no impracticable or dangerous proj-
ects. It does affirm, with an emphasis that must be final,
the irrevocable death of slavery and the true solution to
the problem of peace.

Who Wrote the Message?

There have been questions at times of the authorship of
certain documents which bear the name of the President.
The original manuscript of the Inaugural, fairly covered
with interlinations in the handwriting of Mr. Seward, is
still in existence in Washington. The concluding sentence
of the Emancipation proclamation is known to have been
Mr. Chase's. The purely departmental parts of one or more
late Messages were originally written by other hands.

But the document which, linked with another great act,
will go down to History as having made this a day to be
marked in the calendar beside that one which gives us the
Emancipation Proclamation, is of no uncertain origin. The
more important parts of it were heard by the Cabinet,
when for the first time read to them, in silent approbation.
Not a change of a sentence or a word was suggested. And,
if History wants any Boswellian particulars, it may be

interesting to put in print the fact that the President wrote the Message on stiff sheets of a sort of cardboard, which he could lay upon his knee and write upon as he sat with his feet on the table and his chair tilted back in the "American attitude."

The omission in the President's Message of any allusions to our relations with Great Britain and France has been widely noticed; but it is only a part of the most striking peculiarity which separates this from all previous documents of the kind in our history—a peculiarity which may be best explained by saying that is the most purely *American* message ever delivered to Congress. . . .

Nothing so magnificently independent in the line of State papers has before been done. The whole Continent of America is embraced; save as to the telegraph and the increasing emigration, there is scarcly a reference to the great Powers to which we have been hitherto thought to depend.

Blair's Visit to Richmond*

1865, January 30

The Richmond *Sentinel* of the 28th says: "The late mission of F. B. Blair has naturally excited public curios-

---

* This selection, one of Reid's telegraphic dispatches, appeared in the *Gazette* of January 31, 1865 under the standard title of "Washington Telegraphs." Most such dispatches did not contain as much opinion as this one.

ity. Many vague surmises have been indulged in as to its objects, and some have not only assumed that it relates to a termination of the war between the Confederate States and the United States, but have undertaken to state explicitly the terms upon which the olive branch has been extended by the latter." Thus, the [Cincinnati] *Enquirer* of Thursday says that "nothing has been accomplished toward an immediate peace. We feel justified in assuring our readers that the enemy are willing to permit us to dictate our own terms, provided only that we will not dissolve the Union; guarantee to slavery any constitutional provision for its protection and extension; full compensation in greenbacks for all the negroes that have been carried off during the war; anything, everything that we can ask or think will be freely granted, if only we will consent to reunite with them. These may not have been exactly Mr. Blair's terms, but they embrace the substance of his mission, and do not in the least exaggerate the extremity which the enemy are willing to concede to us if we only return to the Union."

We are at a loss to know how the *Enquirer* reaches the conclusions as to the dispositions of the enemy. They are not warranted by any official or semi-official declaration of the United States Government. On the contrary, the executive head of that Government, in his message of December last, repeated the oft-declared determination of that despotism to be content with nothing short of the abolition of slavery and submission of the South. We cannot too strongly caution the public to beware of the acceptance of every idle rumor as an established truth, concerning this so-called Blair mission. Whatever it looks to, or whatever it means, it may be assumed that at a proper time all the facts relating to it will be made known, if indeed there should be anything worth knowing. The great business of the country is war, and to that business we should address ourselves with renewed purpose and reanimated resolve to achieve our independence.

Lee and Beauregard

1865, February 20

While the guns thunder from the surrounding forts their noisy welcome to conquered Charleston, the more thoughtful begin to tremble before a new danger.

Beauregard is steadily retreating, yet he is known to have thirty-five thousand troops. He makes no serious effort to resist Sherman's advance, defends no river lines, avails himself of no natural advantages, keeping out merely a flying corps of observation on Sherman's front and flanks, he falls steadily and rapidly back. Must it not be for a purpose?

When McClellan was withdrawn from the Peninsula, few will have forgotten how narrowly we escaped irretrievable disaster. Lee, reinforced by Stonewall Jackson, stood between our two armies—an overmatch for either alone. While we sought to unite them, he hurled himself upon one, drove it from Cedar Mountain to Culpepper, to Manassas Junction, to Bull Run; and at last left it cowering beneath the guns that defended Washington itself. Today he stands again between two armies of ours; and for

Stonewall Jackson he has Beauregard marching on interior
lines to reinforce his. It is utterly out of our power to
prevent that reinforcement. With it, Lee is as strong as
Grant and stronger than Sherman. What is there, then, to
save us from a repetition of the second Bull Run campaign?

This only—that George B. McClellan does not command
either of our armies; and that there is no Fitz-John Porter
interested in achieving disaster, intrusted with the power
to secure it.

Undoubtedly sound military science now requires the
rebel evacuation of Richmond to the end of effecting the
speediest junction with Beauregard and forcing a decisive
battle outside of earthworks with one or other of the
National armies. Whether Lee can abandon his persistent
resolution not to fight outside of Virginia, or whether the
rebel authorities feel their condition so desperate as to
demand their desperate remedy of giving up their capital in
order to unite their armies, are other question.

But this much is certain: Lee and Beauregard have it in
their power to unite and fall upon either Sherman or Grant
before these last can by any possibility effect *their* junction. Grant might indeed pursue hastily, but only a combination of favorable circumstances could enable him to be
so close on Lee's heels as to give Sherman effective aid.
Meantime Schofield and Terry, advancing from the coast
towards Raleigh, would be precisely in the way of either
Beauregard or Lee. It is known that here is the point in the
military outlook which General Grant regards with anxious
eyes; and military men at the Capital more than share the
anxiety. Carry us safely past this point, and the spring that
is soon to see our bloodiest battle shall see with it the end
of the rebellion.

On to Richmond!

1865, April 4
From the "Late Headquarters Army
of the James in Front of Fort Harrison"

That was the magnificent war cry of the Nation (fitly voiced by a true exponent of the Nation's wish) which first showed how far their Government in its timorous entrance on civil war lagged behind THE PEOPLE. Withdrawn in a moment of unutterable public cowardice, induced by a disaster springing wholly from imbecile delay, it was followed by years of maundering drivel called Strategy; by campaigns that wasted the armies of the Republic that a General might be made President—perhaps of the whole, perhaps of a fragment—of the struggling Nation; by games of "blindfold" in which we stumbled about to seek for fit leaders; and at last by the remorseless devastation of the war in earnest, which these insane delays had made necessary.

After nearly two years more of such struggling—on the very anniversary of the day on which the Peace Convention ended its fruitless sessions—four years to a day after Ex-President John Tyler had made his defiant speech in Washington proclaiming the dissolution of the Union and demanding the recognition of the seceding States as one of the Independent Powers of the earth—less by a couple of weeks than four years from the firing of the first shot by an insurgent force against the flag of the Government—the Secretary of War—fit spokesman for such a message now—announces from the portico of the War Office that the Government of the insurgents is scattered and RICH-MOND IS OURS!

And so, once again, the Press raises the cry "On to Richmond!"

Washington was aflame with its triumphant glow. The War office was surrounded with a great multitude clamoring for more news, cheering, waving hats, singing "Rally Round the Flag," embracing each other, and making the most formidable efforts to embrace—Stanton! "I forgive ye all yer sins, ye old blizzard!" shouted a jubilant soldier at the Secretary; while Seward shook him by the hand till the radical and conservative had melted into one in the nervous, spasmodic grin; and tears stood in Stanton's eyes as he turned from one to another to acknowledge the rush of blood-hot congratulations that had suddenly transformed him—revival though it was of the age of miracles—into the most popular man in Washington!

Foreign ministers were hurrying to the State Department with their congratulations; the Secretaries were giving holidays to their armies of clerks and vainly trying to make speeches enough to furnish fit answer to the endless volleys of cheers; processions, headed by the omnipresent Stars and Stripes, suddenly sprang out of chaos on the streets; every glimpse of bunting with the Red, White and Blue was cheered as it passed to the echo; Ben Butler was summoned from the hotel to receive the homage of the vast crowd that hailed him as organizer and author of the army that took Richmond; Vice President Johnson, sober as to his stomach but amazingly excited and even incoherent as to his head, was making speeches from Admiral Lee's door steps, from Montgomery Blair's door steps, from the hotel piazzas; the faces of the negroes yawned into vast caverns of red, bounded by ivory, while the more sedate managed to exclaim to one another amid their shakings and chucklings, "I say, Sam, d'ye hear, de niggahs tuck Richmond"; the crowds blocked the streets till our carriage could hardly force its way through them to the wharf of the boat for City Point.

Aboard, the scene was scarcely less tumultuous. Every man insisted on every other man's straightway bolting brandy and whisky in alternate swallows in interminable succession; and it really required a good deal of self denial to resist. Carl Schurz was in the crowd, nervous and restless, because steam couldn't make faster time. He had just procured an assignment to duty under Sherman, and here the war was going to end before he could get into the field. Francis Channing Barlow, boy and Major General with the scars of half a dozen surgical pronounced mortal wounds upon him, was hurrying direct from the last Cunard steamer to get into the field again to see the last of it. A swarm of officers, recalled by the army's triumphs from half expired furloughs or just exchanged from rebel prisons were eager to catch up with their commands before the final struggle. And, to be sure there were not wanting men who wanted trade permits for stores in Richmond, and sutlers who must hurry their stock up to Richmond, and Quartermaster's clerks, who thought they could make money in Richmond; and all the myriad formed parasites that feed upon great armies, who wanted to dig for money around the garbage of Richmond.

The occasion, of course, had brought out the Press. I encountered on board the boat my old friend, L. L. Crounse, night editor of the New York *Times* whom I last met in the field at Gettysburg; C. A. Page of the *Tribune* was there, worthily reenacting the *Tribune's* war cry; and below we heard were Richard T. Colbern of the *World,* [and]

Coffin of the *Boston Journal*. So were to meet in the rebel capital, so many of the "Old Guard" of Army Correspondents, who four years ago had met in the young romance of the war in the fields of the Southwest.

The band played the National airs, the forts along the Potomac thundered out their stormy salutes, Mount Vernon gleamed in a passing glimpse of sunshine from its green eminence, Acquia Creek was deserted, the Potomac flotilla was idle or absent—its occupation gone—and so we steamed out into the night and the Chesapeake.

One by one the enthusiasts yielded to unstrung nerves and disappeared; till all were quiet, all but one—a wretch whose stentorian and stertorous snore invaded all ears. Toward morning endurance ceased to be a virtue, and a Yankee near the offender shouted, "I sa-ay, stranger ca-an't you mo-ove that nose o' yourn?" Other remonstrances came to reinforce the Yankee; and presently, behold a righteous retribution! The wretch was so thoroughly awaked that he got up to look around. In an instant the pitching of the waves had made him seasick and with a rush to the bow, he began the literary work known as "contributions to the Atlantic." He troubled *us* no more!

1865, April 5
From Spottswood House, Richmond, Va.

There had been suggestions of guerrillas last night, and Moseby had been significantly named in connection with the fact that not even an outpost of the army was nearer to us than Richmond. But we curled up on her sofas in the blankets the negroes had brought before the roaring fire they had kindled and laughed Moseby to scorn. We were right.

This morning good old rebel aunties's coffee and bacon were ready at the moment, and with an extra stirrup cup for ourselves and all the loose change in our pockets for the picanninnies, we were off for Richmond.

Richmond

The morning clouds began to clear away, as a turn in the road brought an exclamation to all lips. Before us, amid the rising mists, were the spires of Richmond. To the left, reminding one of Richelieu's description of the Bastille, "Where the clouds of heaven hung the blackest," was a slowly rising smoke, that as we afterward learned, very accurately marked the position of the Libby [prison]. . . .

Squalid houses, tow-head children, the poverty and degradation of the outcasts of a great city were not unusual things to observe. Beyond these, there was nothing save here and there the protrusion from some filthy hovel of a flagstaff with the Stars and Stripes.

At last our ambulance drew up before the Spottswood. Somewhat to my astonishment, I confess, the rebel landlord stood in the office. "I want a private parlor and bedroom attached." "Certainly; will be delighted to accomodate you." I had the pleasure of registering my name below a swarm of rebel officers—the first arrival direct from Washington or the North. A negro waiter seized the baggage and seemed to me a trifle more attentive than eyes of mine every beheld negro before.

The rooms were as good as the Continental or Fifth
Avenue would have given—except that the furniture, car-
pets and curtains were all at least four years old. The
African wasn't satisfied till my boots were cleaned and the
soiled linen handed over—"washed and ironed in six hours,
Massah!" On the whole, the Spottswood seems to be a
very fair house!

The flag under which Washington served once more
floated above his statue on the State House Square; a
Yankee band was playing the National airs; negroes had
violated the unwritten law of the Capital and invaded the
sacred common; cavalry guidons were in front of the
Executive Mansion of the Governor of Virginia; staff officers crowded the portico; and headquarters of General
Charles Devens an oldtime New England Democrat,
commanding the white troops in the city, were within.
These were the first points one observed in sallying out
from the Spottswood to look at Richmond. . . .

The Burnt District

If Cincinnati were to be burnt clean from Third street
down to the river and from Western Row up the river to
Pendleton, it would have lost about as much in proportion
to its size as Richmond has by General Ewell's pleasant
diversion. Within the burnt district were located the whole-
sale stores, the tobacco warehouses, most of the great
mills, many of the banks, some of the newspaper offices;
in short, it embraced nearly all the heavy business of the
city together with many of the squalid tenement houses of
the poorer classes.

All the aristocratic portion of the city, above and to the

westward of the State House, is unharmed. From the hill beyond First Street looking out upon the Bell Island and the rapids of the James, . . .far as the eye can reach stretch the fertile bottom lands that border the James, green with the growing wheat, and bounded on either side with undulating, forest-crowned, hill sides, amid which may be distinguished the fine old Virginian mansions. To the left is a beautiful city, rich in the stores of great cities (richer in its fair women and brave men), richest in its ancestral stories and noble history, that all the last four years must not, cannot blot out.

And in front where should be the very flower and final concentration of this city's wealth and growth—one vast, unbroken stretch of ruins, crumbing walls, yawning doorways, tottering steeples. Richmond is today a city of aristocratic residences, without the business heart that should support them—it is the glowing cheek, the rippling hair, the sparkling eye of a glorious woman, without one pulsation of the blood that should feed these beauties.

The Negroes

Nothing could be better than the behavior of the negroes. Some of the citizens, who "hate a d____d nigger anyhow," complain of their having been riotous during the fire, but I found no evidence to show that they had behaved nearly so badly as some of the whites. Others complain that they have become "saucy"; but this too is rather what they feel bound to believe must be, than what they actually see.

Here at the Spottswood House the negroes—all slaves two days ago, all free now and knowing that they are free—continue quietly at their regular work. The proprietor complains that during the fire on Monday he could get nothing done; but with such a fire raging all around them, servants in any house would scarcely be very attentive. To night the hotel is overruning with officers who have at last worked their way from City Point; yet, in the midst of such confusion, no hotel could show better attention to the wants of its guests than these liberated slaves are giving.

Throughout the city, the majority of them are thus far remaining quietly with their late masters at their old duties. They all know they are free and chuckle greatly over the thought; but they mean to give their masters a chance to pay them wages.

The first thing many ask about is the prospect for negro schools. They have heard in some way that in other cities the advent of the Yankees was the signal for beginning the education of themselves and their children; and they are anxiously awaiting the same result here.

For the most part, I doubt if the inferior classes of slaves very well understand yet what it all means. "It don't tak no more passes now to go around nowhar," exclaimed a burly black a moment ago to his comrade beneath the window. That seems to be as far as many of them get. They know that they can go about without passes, that they can smoke cigars in the State House square, and stay out after nine o'clock if they wish; and they have a vague sort of jubilant feeling about being free, but I doubt if many of them realize that freedom means simply work for themselves.

Of course they are all our friends; all cheer the flag and

listen to the music and glorify the Yankees. They are very proud of our negro soldiers; say that the rebel attempt to arm them wouldn't work; and declare that they got none into their companies except such as were forced in.

The Poor Whites

One does not see very much of the poorer classes of whites. A few women are groping piteously among the smoldering ruins, and a few laboring men go listlessly about the streets; but the numbers are fewer than would be expected. They seem to hate the negroes; but their dislike to their late rebel masters is even more emphatic; and altogether they appear ready to bear the negroes for the sake of getting back under a settled Government. They complain in a tone of almost fierceness that the fire disclosed an abundance of provision in the warehouses of the speculators and talk bitterly about the rigors of the conscription. A few are open Unionists; of the rest, the most have a sort of sulky satisfaction in being back again under the old flag.

The citizens of foreign birth are nearly all more or less openly on our side.

The Ruling Classes

On arriving here I could think of but two Richmond families of any prominence in which I could claim an acquaintance. One of them was that of the former rebel

Secretary of War; and I was scarcely surprised to find that of it not a single member remained.

I called on the other this evening. I have no right to give the name; but it is one not merely of old Virginia repute, but even of national fame. One of its members is the owner of a magnificent plantation on the James. The advance of our armies drove him to the town residence of the family, where I found them all gathered.

That I was courteously and even hospitably received— abolitionist though I was known to be—need hardly be said; but the defiant spirit with which even the ladies bore up under the crushing loss of their Capital was to me at once something very wonderful and indeed admirable.

"Richmond ought to have been given up long ago," said a rebellious fair one of the family. "It would have been far better for our cause and would have insured its return to us all the sooner."

"But, surely," I interrupted, "you cannot imagine that your armies will ever regain Richmond?"

"Ah, sir," she responded, with a knowing smile, "What news do they have at your headquarters this evening? Perhaps you don't know that Johnston has joined Lee with his whole force? And, indeed," she added, half confidently, half inquiringly, "I'm not sure but there's better news than all that."

"You forget," I suggested, "that, even if you were right in your news, your cause would still be hopeless from sheer want of numbers."

"Ah, that's what you have told us already so many times. *You* forget that we have seen dark days before. The same God that delivered us then will protect and save us now!" And she clasped her hands over her breast with a wild, imploring gesture, that, in spite of her confident speech, showed how ill at ease she still was.

"I must tell you, though," said another lady of the family, "how disappointed we all have been at the conduct of your soldiers. Indeed, it has been admirable; and I am sorry to believe that the discipline of your army must be better than that of ours."

If these had been mere vulgar trimmers, anxious to curry favor with the winning side, this would have been worthless; but coming from the haughtiest and most defiant rebels, it was beyond price.

The town is full of such people. Many rebels who had occupied high official positions are still here unable to get away. Some have manifested equal pluck and confidence; with others, it has seemed to me only a vain bravado. Still others frankly admit that their cause is lost, and profess to be ready to adapt themselves to circumstances. But with none is the submission other than sullen or forced. I have conversed with dozens of them today; but I have neither seen nor heard of one who was really an honest Unionist. Loyalty in Richmond must be sought outside the "upper classes."

Edward A. Pollard, the rebel historian, and associate editor of the *Examiner,* is here at the Spottswood, rather despondent, and a little bit seedy in appearance. Another who has just turned up, is Mr. A. Judson Crane, whom Mr. Lincoln thought a good enough Unionist in 1861 to be appointed District Attorney. "I wept four years ago when I saw the old flag hauled down," said he this morning, "and I tell you the truth, I wept a great deal harder the other day when I saw it go up again." Quite a number of others expressed the same sentiment in almost identical language.

April, 1865*

1865, April 19

Historic Nineteenth of April! This day, four years ago, in the streets of Baltimore, the first blood was shed in the War for the Union; this day, after four years of terrible war amid bulletins of falling cities and surrendering armies, the Rebellion ends, and the authorities of the Nation, in all the pomp and circumstance of funeral grief, bear from the White House to the Capitol with crape-enshrouded banners, and muffled drums, and arms reversed, and cannon shrouded, and mournful martial music, and a long, long procession,   "As fits an universal woe,"

the murdered martyr, whose tragic death closes the War, and opens the reconstruction.

"Bury the great man
With an empire's lamentation,

---

* This Agate letter not in the Reid Collection appeared in the *Gazette* April 26, 1865. The poem is from Alfred Lord Tennyson's "Ode on the Death of the Duke of Wellington"from which Reid selected a few lines and changed a few words.

Let us bury the great man
To the noise of the mourning of a mighty nation."

"Mourning when its leaders fall;
While sorrow adornes hamlet and hall.

"Mourn for the man of amplest influence,
Yet clearest of ambitious crime,
Our foremost, yet with least pretense;

"Rich in saving common sense,
And, as the greatest only are,
In his simplicity sublime."

Index

Entries in bold face refer to Volume II

Entries in bold face refer to Volume II

Brooks, Noah, 8
Browning, Mrs. Elizabeth B., 123
Brownlow, Parson William G., 163
Brown's Gap, VA, 178
Bruce, Col. Saunders D., 156, 161
Buchanan, Pres. James, 124
Buckland, Col. Ralph P., 126, 128, 131, 133-35
Buckner, Brig. Gen. Simon B., C.S.A., 69, 71-76, 87, 101, 111, 114, 186, 228
Buell, Gen. Don Carlos, 92-93, 101-03, 105, 115-16, 121-22, 139, 146, 149-51, 153, 155, 158, 161-62, 171, 188, 160, 181
Buford, Brig. Gen. John, 26, 28
Bull Run, 111, 131, Second Bull Run, 207, 216; 220, 230, 254, 259, 8, 155, 191-92
Bull Town, WV, 44
Burlingame, Sgt., 35
Burnside, Gen. Ambrose E., 241-42, 139, 155
Butler, Benjamin, 86, 153-54, 178, 194
Butterfield, Gen. Daniel, 64

C

Cacapon River, WV, 64, 66
Cairo, IL, 105-10, 193

Caldwell, Brig. Gen. John C., 38
Cameron, Simon, Secy. of War, 83-86, 162, 168-70
Camp Dennison, OH, 25, 70
Camp Dick Robinson, KY, 69, 70, 78, 89, 100, 187
Camp Nevin, KY, 80, 179, 186
Camp Nolin, KY, 78, 187
Canfield, Col. Herman, 128, 135
Canton, KY, 110
Cape Hatteras, NC, 239, 241
Carleton Publishing Co., 184
Carnifex Ferry, WV, 11, 42, 58-60, 182-83
Carrick's Ford, WV, 11, 28, 35, 27
Carrington, Adj. Gen. Henry B., 14
Casey, Samuel, M.C., 274, 92
Cavender, Maj. John S., 145
Cedar Creek, VA, 179-80, 182
Cedar Mountain, VA, 191
Cedarville, OH, 3
Cemetery Hill, 24-26, 29, 33-37, 39-42, 49-50, 52, 57, 60-61, 67
Centreville, VA, 218-19, 224
Chain Bridge, D.C., 218
Chambersburg, PA, 1, 21
Chambers Creek, TN, 190
Chancellorsville, VA, 207, 260, 269, 17, 19, 26-27, 139, 155
Chaplin Hills, KY, 89, 100
Charleston, S.C., 240, 260
Charleston, WV, 61, 173, 191
Charleston Harbor, SC, 258-59

Entries in bold face refer to Volume II

Entries in bold face refer to Volume II

Entries in bold face refer to Volume II

Entries in bold face refer to Volume II

Entries in bold face refer to Volume II

Entries in bold face refer to Volume II

Entries in bold face refer to Volume II

Entries in bold face refer to Volume II

Entries in bold face refer to Volume II

134-35, 138-40, 148, 156,
163n, 177, 181, 245, 77-79,
83, 92-93, 93n, 108, 127,
127n, 128-29, 162-63, 167,
171, 177, 180, 182
Ohio Abolitionists, 41
Ohio Regiments, 11, 14-15, 23,
36, 61, 101, 34, First, 156;
Fourth, Company H, 14;
Sixth, 156; Seventh, 10;
Tenth, 48-49, 53, Company
A,B,C,E, 51; Twelfth, 51, 53;
Thirteenth, 51-52, 57, 156,
163; Fourteenth, 29, 32-35,
67-68; Twentieth, 157;
Twenty-fourth, 156; Forty-
first, 156; Forty-sixth, 128;
Forth-eighth, 121, 128, 135;
Forty-ninth, 157; Fifty-third,
128, 130; Fifty-fourth, 138;
Fifty-sixth, 157; Fifty-eighth,
157; Fifty-ninth, 128, 156;
Sixty-eighth, 157; Seventieth,
121, 128; Seventy-first, 138-
40; Seventy-second, 121, 128,
135; Seventy-sixth, 157, 169;
Seventy-seventh, 128; Seventy-
eighth, 157
Ohio River, 45, 64, 71, 187,
156, 181
Ohio State Journal, 6
Oliver, Maj. John M., 165
Opequan, VA, 177
Orange and Alexandria Railroad,
131

Oregon, 210

P

Page, Charles A., correspondent
for New York *Tribune,* 8, 195
Painter, Uriah H., 7
Pamunky River, VA, 157
Parkersburg, WV, 46
Parrott, Col. Edward A., 156
Parsons, Lt. Charles C., 164
Passaic, 240
Patrick, Gen. Marsena R., 14-15
Patterson's Creek, WV, 63
PawPaw, WV, 63-64
Pea Ridge, AR, 156
Pease, Col. Phineas, 134
Peckham, Lt. Col. James, 157
Pendleton, George H., 83
Penisula Campaign, 209, 211,
217, 156, 191
Pennsylvania, 157, 1-2, 4-5, 10,
13, 18, 31-33, 62, 76, 80, 84,
90, 115, 162, 164, 166, 170
Pennsylvania Dutch, 20-22
Pennsylvania Regiments, 31-32
Seventy-seventh, 157
Perry, Oliver H., 73
Perryville, KY, 89, 93, 100, 102
Petersburg, VA, 177
Pfyffe, Col. James P., 128, 156
Philadelphia, PA, 200, 1, 3, 12,
46, 67, 96-97, 121, 126, 172-
73

Entries in bold face refer to Volume II

Entries in bold face refer to Volume II

Entries in bold face refer to Volume II

Entries in bold face refer to Volume II

Taneytown, MD, 13, 16, 18-19,
26, 34-37, 54
Taylor's Chicago Light Artillery,
(Lt. Walter J. Taylor), 135
Taylor, Zachery, 69
Telegraphic *Dispatches*, 2, 6, 74,
74n, 75, 92-93, 93n, 94, 94n,
109-11, 189, 189n, 190-91
Tennessee, 4-5, 24, 73, 75-78,
105, 107, 112, 114-15, 119,
127, 163, 180n, 189, 261,
**104, 106, 117, 133, 137-38,
145, 163, 167, 170, 172**
Tennessee-East, 60, 71, 77, 101,
112, **76, 150, 167**
Tennessee and Lynchburg Rail-
road, 60
Tennessee River, 139
Tennessee River Expedition,
119-20, 149
Tennyson, Alfred Lord, **204n**
Terrill, Capt. William R., 162
Terry, Brig. Gen. Alfred H., 192
Texas, 106, 117, **150**
Thayer, Col. John M., 157
Thomas, Benjamin F., M.C., 93
Thomas, Gen. George H., 141-
42, 148, 181
Thomas, Gen. Lorenzo, 101,
185-87
Thompson, Capt. Noah S., 157,
167
Thoroughfare Gap, VA, 220
Thurber, Lt. Charles H., 157,
167

Thruston, Gen. Gates P., **132n,
133n**
Tousseau, Gen. Lovell H., **156**
Tremain, Lyman, M.C., 170
Trimble, Carey A., M.C., 92
Truesdail, William, 146
Tullahoma, TN, **133, 137-38**
Tunnel Hill, TN, **181**
Twiggs, Maj. Gen. David Emanu-
el, C.S.A., 86
Two Taverns, PA, 13, 21, 56
Tyler, Gen. Erastus B., 10
Tyler Gunboat, 123
Tyler, John, ex-President, 193

U

Union Troops, see Army of the
Potomac, Army of the Cum-
berland; see also various State
Regiments
Union Troops, impression made
on Southerners, 113, **203**
United States Army, (Battal-
ions), Fifteenth, **156**; Six-
teenth, **156**; Nineteenth, **156**
Usher, John P., Secy. Interior,
152

V

Vallandigham, Clement L., 79,
82, 84, 127, 127n, 129-30,
176

Entries in bold face refer to Volume II

Entries in bold face refer to Volume II

Entries in bold face refer to Volume II

DATE DUE